Smithsonian

Q&A

THE ULTIMATE QUESTION
AND ANSWER BOOK

PENGUINS

HarperCollins books may be purchased for educational, business, or sales promotional use. For information, please write: Special Markets Department, HarperCollins Publishers, 10 East 53rd Street, New York, NY 10022.

Produced for HarperCollins by:

 HYDRA PUBLISHING
129 MAIN STREET
IRVINGTON, NY 10533
WWW.HYLASPUBLISHING.COM

FIRST EDITION

The name of the "Smithsonian," "Smithsonian Institution," and the sunburst logo are registered trademarks of the Smithsonian Institution.

Library of Congress Cataloging-in-Publication Data

Davis, Lloyd S.
  Smithsonian Q & A : Penguins : the ultimate question and answer book / Lloyd Spencer Davis. -- 1st ed.
     p. cm.
  Includes bibliographical references.
  ISBN: 978-0-06-089126-8
  ISBN-10: 0-06-089126-2
  1. Penguins--Miscellanea. I. Smithsonian Institution. II. Title. III. Title: Smithsonian question and answer. IV. Title: Penguins.

  QL696.S473D396 2007
  598.47--dc22

                                    2007060871

07   08   09   10   QW   10   9   8   7   6   5   4   3   2   1

Smithsonian

Q&A

THE ULTIMATE QUESTION
AND ANSWER BOOK

PENGUINS

Lloyd Spencer Davis

Collins
An Imprint of HarperCollinsPublishers

PENGUINS

Contents

Magellanic Penguins
perform a duet.

Adelie Penguins in an Antarctic snowstorm.

A distinctive white patch and bright red beak readily identify the Gentoo Penguin.

THE WONDERFUL WORLD OF PENGUINS

Evolution is a wonderful thing: it has given us dinosaurs and orchids, hummingbirds and pandas. That life could progress from soup to cell to us defies comprehension. That it could also produce penguins seems both baffling and a blessing.

Penguins are birds, but they are like no other birds. They are as distinct as any group of animals can be: only penguins get recognized as penguins and penguins are never mistaken for anything else. What was evolution thinking when it made penguins?

We are used to thinking of evolution as a headlong march from simple to complex, from poor to grand, with each new invention added to the rest. Abacus to calculator to computer. Paramecium to earthworm to people. There is almost an inevitability to it, with each shiny new model being better than the one before, more able, more sophisticated.

Left: African Penguins congregate on a beach in South Africa. Contrary to popular images, not all penguins live in the Antarctic.

Below: Rockhopper Penguins add an unruly yellow crest to the basic black-and-white penguin uniform.

But penguins fly in the face of that—or rather, more to the point, they do not. They seem to have reversed evolution's trends. They are birds but they have given up flight, the one huge advantage that birds have over most of the other large animals. It would be like ordering the latest model Cadillac only to discover that it comes without an engine: it is back to the Flintstones and pedal-power for you.

It seems a strange thing for penguins to do but, in fact, they have taken the concept of turning back evolution's clock much further. Penguins give the impression that they would be happy to jump in a time machine and go back 400 million years, to a time when the most complex thing in nature was a fish. Penguins, it seems, want to be fish again. Like avian versions of Thoreau, they seek a simpler life—except they want to live in the pond, not beside it.

Why? It is a reasonable question with a simple answer: life at sea looked to be easier than life on land. This was before evolution had even gotten around to thinking about seals and whales. The sea it seems was teeming with fish and other edibles. Furthermore, there was nowhere for the prey to hide in open water. The trouble for the would-be penguins, however, was that the sea did have depth, and their prey could run, or at least swim as fast as their little caudal fins could take them, to depths beyond the reach of any flying bird.

A Chinstrap Penguin on the subantarctic Half Moon Island.

King Penguins take a swim. Penguins are adapted to a life at sea.

The solution? Ditch flight, which required large fragile wings and light bodies, and become a submarine, which meant having short powerful flippers and a body shape that was more Buddha than budgerigar. Yet, that in itself was not enough to succeed at sea. Sixty-odd million years ago, when the first prototype penguins were being wheeled out of evolution's factories, attention had to be paid to many more details.

For one thing, water is a lot denser than air: to move through it efficiently meant having a streamlined body and, amazingly, no body shape in the animal kingdom—indeed, no shape designed by humans either—has a lower coefficient of drag (a measure of how streamlined it is) than a penguin's body. Okay to a point, but there is not much value in being able to move efficiently through water if you cannot stay in it long and, in that regard, penguins had one major design problem to solve that fish did not have to deal with: they were warm-blooded.

Running the engine hot has huge advantages for animals that need to move quickly to catch prey or avoid being eaten themselves: chemical reactions occur more quickly, muscles contract more quickly, the animals move more quickly. It is why the Age of Dinosaurs was always going to give way to the Age of Mammals, come comets or high water. Birds, like mammals, are warm-blooded, which means that to function properly they must maintain their core body temperatures irrespective of the temperatures around them. Not such a big problem on land, but a huge one when in water because water acts as a heat sink, sucking warmth from the body at about 25 times the rate that heat is lost in air. To become a truly aquatic creature, penguins needed some sort of insulation if their design concept was to have flippers, so to speak.

The solution was ingenious: make use of the feathers that come with every bird. They trebled their density, shortened them, and created a watertight covering by having the feathers lock to each other with little hooks. At their base, long downy filaments provided the loft and the trapped air the insulation. This was the Thermos flask, it was double-glazing, and all invented sixty million years ago.

But the birds were not out of trouble yet; their feather survival suits presented other difficulties that evolution had to solve. As effective as these personal duvets were at keeping out the cold, there was a problem with the building materials: feathers wear out. Like tires on a car, feathers must be replaced to remain effective. This has meant that penguins can never be free of the land from where they came: they must return to it to molt. During the process of molt, old feathers are pushed out by new ones growing underneath and, for a period in this state of undress, the penguins are deprived of the insulation that would enable them to survive at sea.

Of course, it is not just molt that prevents penguins from completely turning back time and becoming like fish again: they must get out of the water to breed, too. Their eggs and chicks must be kept warm. Whales managed to kiss the land good-bye completely when they too followed penguins back into the sea but, as mammals, they already had

internal gestation whereby the young could be nurtured and kept warm inside the mother's own underwater life support system. Such an option was not available for penguins; evolution could only work with the materials at its disposal and, because birds laid porous eggs that had to be kept warm, there was no alternative: penguins had to breed upon land. So the penguins we see are the penguins on land, where they seem to be compromised by all the design changes that were needed for life at sea. They walk funny. They look like they are wearing tuxedos. Mom and dad must both work together to rear the offspring and, as a consequence—for sound if somewhat prosaic evolutionary reasons—they all look very similar.

It is easy to mock penguins. To laugh at them when they trip. To dismiss them as all being the same. To see them in the Antarctic (one of the benefits of their excellent insulation for life in water is that even the coldest temperatures on land are bearable) and presume that they are creatures of the snow and ice. To see them in colonies in their thousands and presume that they are immune to the changes we have wrought upon the world. But in these observations, and nearly everything else we assume about penguins, we would be wrong.

One thing we do get right is our affection for penguins. They may be one of evolution's weirdest creations, but they are lovable with it. This is not so much the wonderful world of penguins as it is a world made more wonderful by penguins.

The aptly named Little Penguins are the smallest of the penguins.

CHAPTER 1

PENGUIN HISTORY

T here are few creatures on Earth more universally loved than penguins, no creatures more instantly recognizable. From the plains of Arkansas to the headwaters of the Zambesi River, people the world over know penguins—even though the vast majority have never seen a real penguin, and probably never will. But what do we really know about this animal that we have taken into our hearts, if not our heads? Penguins are in danger of becoming caricatures of themselves. The cartoonists have commandeered them as their icons for conformity and uniformity, for funny and awkward, for snow and ice. They walk like us. They swim like fish. They seem cute and cuddly. The reality, however, is that real penguins are not like that at all. They are surprisingly varied, remarkably agile, and they can be found living in deserts in some of the hottest climates of the world. Real penguins can be aggressive and their coats are stiff, unlike the soft, fluffy coverings of toy penguins. Most of all, appearances to the contrary, they are neither mammals nor fish: penguins are birds.

Above: A penguin that never goes near ice, the Snares Penguin breeds only on the tiny Snares Islands south of New Zealand.

Left: The classic view of penguins: a Gentoo Penguin stands before the icebergs of Antarctica.

Penguins Are Birds

African Penguins, like these on the beaches of South Africa, were the first penguins encountered by explorers from the Northern Hemisphere.

Q: What is a penguin?

A: Penguins are birds, from the eggs in which they begin their lives to the tips of their feathers. It is true that they do not fly, but flight is not a defining characteristic of birds: feathers and their type of eggs are. Birds probably evolved from dinosaurs—technically, some would argue, they should still be classified as dinosaurs—and principal among the design changes that enabled them to lift off from the Earth's surface was the evolution of feathers and becoming warm-blooded. Maintaining a high body temperature enabled the chemical reactions that turn food into energy to occur more efficiently, but it also meant that birds had eggs that needed to be incubated. The ability to fly brought so many advantages to birds, it is hard to imagine why any bird would want to give that up. Penguins, it turns out, are the only family of waterbirds in which all members are flightless. In the language of scientists, their family is called Spheniscidae, which means "little wedge," but to the rest of us, they are simply "penguins."

It may not look like your average bird, but the feathers and eggs of this Adelie Penguin point to its flying ancestors.

Q: When were penguins first discovered?

A: The native peoples in areas frequented by penguins undoubtedly knew of their existence—and in some cases used them for food—but without written records, it is impossible to say how long ago that association began. The first published account of penguins came from a chap aboard Ferdinand Magellan's famous first circumnavigation of the world: Antonio Pigafetta described catching penguins on January 27, 1520, near what was probably Punta Tombo in Argentina, which even today is the site of a very large Magellanic penguin colony. Except that Pigafetta did not call them penguins, he called them "geese." But really, the first recorded encounter with penguins came from another famous voyage: Vasco da Gama's rounding of Cape Horn. On November 25, 1497, the expedition stopped at what is now called Mossel Bay in South Africa and an anonymous diarist wrote, "there are birds as big as ducks, but they cannot fly . . . and they bray like asses." This could only describe African Penguins, which continue to live in Mossel Bay, and are also known as "Jackass Penguins" because of their donkeylike braying. The diary did not get published until 1838 (hence, it was Pigafetta's account that first alerted the world to the existence of penguins) and, somewhat prescient of the sailors that would come after him, the Portuguese recorder of these observations ascribed to the penguins what apparently was a name by which the Great Auk was known.

Q: Why are they called penguins?

A: "Penguin" was yet another one of the names given to the Great Auk, a flightless and now-extinct member of the family of birds, Alcidae, that includes auks and puffins. When sailors from the Northern Hemisphere encountered flightless black-and-white seabirds near the bottom of Argentina, they transferred the name "penguin" to them. This was late in the sixteenth century.

Q: Are penguins related to auks?

A: No . . . well, only inasmuch as all birds are more related to some extent than they are to, say, dogs. Auks and puffins constitute an entirely separate family of birds from that of penguins. The superficial physical similarities of auks and penguins result not from descent from a common ancestor, but from a process known as convergent evolution. Because they have similar ways of life (both are diving seabirds feeding on small fish and the like), evolution has come to shape them in similar ways. What makes the squat streamlined body shape adaptive to an auk also makes it adaptive to a penguin; what makes the black back and white front of a penguin advantageous for chasing fish also makes it advantageous for auks. The thing is, auks live in the Northern Hemisphere.

Leaving aside the fact that it can fly, the Razorbill, a medium-sized alcid, looks superficially like a penguin. Its similar appearance, however, is a result not of common ancestry, but of convergent evolution.

I have often had the impression that, to penguins, man is just another penguin—different, less predictable, occasionally violent, but tolerable company when he sits still and minds his own business.
—BERNARD STONEHOUSE, AUTHOR OF THE LAST CONTINENT: DISCOVERING ANTARCTICA

Where Penguins Live

Q: Where do penguins live?

A: Penguins live only in the Southern Hemisphere, but they occupy a surprisingly large part of it. They are quite literally the world's only 100-degree birds, breeding in climates that range from −75°F to +104°F (−60°C to +40°C). They breed farther south than any other bird. Not at the South Pole, as misconceptions might have it, but in the Antarctic at Cape Royds, latitude 77°33′S (which, incidentally, is the same place from where Ernest Shackleton made his abortive attempt to walk to the South Pole). They also breed right on the equator in the Galápagos Islands. In between they can be found around South America, southern Africa, Australia, New Zealand, and the islands of the subantarctic.

Q: Does that mean polar bears and penguins are not found together?

A: The likes of Gary Larson have a lot to answer for; despite the common depiction in cartoons of penguins together with polar bears, Eskimos, and igloos, the reality could not be more different. Polar bears, Eskimos, and igloos are found in the Northern Hemisphere; penguins are not.

Above right: Cartoonists refuse to let the facts get in the way of a good drawing; they persist in showing penguins, polar bears, igloos, and Eskimos together.

Right: Penguins are found only in the Southern Hemisphere: around the Antarctic continent and the islands of the subantarctic; New Zealand and the bottom half of Australia; the tip of southern Africa; the sides of South America; and right up to the Galápagos Islands on the equator.

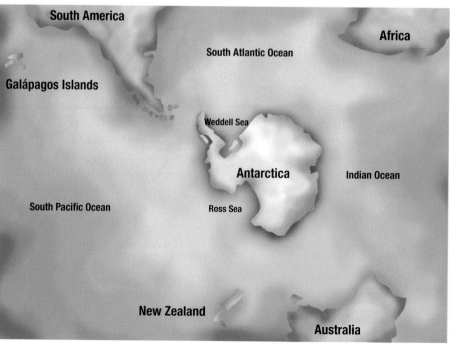

South America

Africa

South Atlantic Ocean

Galápagos Islands

Weddell Sea

Antarctica

Indian Ocean

South Pacific Ocean

Ross Sea

New Zealand

Australia

Q: Why are there no penguins in the Northern Hemisphere?

A: Becoming flightless is something that birds can afford to do only in environments where there are no ground predators. In the Northern Hemisphere, the presence of ground predators such as bears, wolves, and wolverines make flightlessness a less attractive option. Whatever advantages it might bring in terms of diving for food, plump flightless birds living in the Northern Hemisphere are likely to become food themselves. Indeed, extinction has been the fate of the few flightless seabirds that have arisen in the Northern Hemisphere, including the Great Auk.

Of course, predators can include humans: the last two Great Auks known to have existed were killed on the island of Eldey off the coast of Iceland on June 4, 1844. Penguins, on the other hand, evolved in the predator-free areas of the Southern Hemisphere that also gave rise to such other flightless icons as the Kiwi and the Emu, as well as the Cassowary, the Flightless Steamerduck, and the Flightless Cormorant.

Q: Have penguins always lived in the Southern Hemisphere?

A: It would seem that they have. Fossilized penguin remains have been found from South Africa, New Zealand, Australia, and South America to the subantarctic islands and the Antarctic continent: all areas still frequented by penguins.

Q: Where was the first penguin fossil found?

A: In 1848, Walter Mantell—the son of the British doctor, Gideon Mantell, who discovered the first dinosaur fossil—acquired a bone unearthed from Kakanui, New Zealand, that would turn out to be the first penguin fossil. Back in England, Thomas Huxley, Charles Darwin's most ardent supporter, described the tarsometatarsus (fused anklebone) and christened the extinct species to which it belonged, *Palaeeudyptes antarcticus* ("ancient winged diver of the south"). No other specimen has ever been found but, from the age of the limestone deposits around Kakanui, it is likely that *Palaeeudyptes* lived somewhere between 23 to 34 million years ago and was estimated to stand about four feet tall.

Big and vulnerable: both are consequences of becoming flightless and the reasons the Great Auk is no more. Although similar in appearance, Great Auks were not close relatives of penguins.

Penguin Evolution

Q: When did penguins first evolve?

A: North from Kakanui on the east coast of New Zealand's South Island is a place called Waipara. It is an area noted for the wines its soils produce, but those same soils have also produced a few fragments of flipper and shoulder bones belonging to the world's oldest-known penguin. Dated at 60 million years old, this bird had characteristics that were clearly those of a diving penguin, while still retaining some of the more fragile aspects of a flying bird's anatomy. So, about 60 million years ago, give or take a millennium or two, seems as close as we are likely to get to pinpointing that moment—as significant to penguins as was the moment when our ancestors first stood up and walked on two legs—when a group of flightless diving birds evolved and forevermore their descendants would be known as penguins.

Christened *Waimanu manneringi*, this is a reconstruction of the earliest-known penguin, which lived in the shallow seas off New Zealand about 60 million years ago. *Waimanu* penguins were probably about the size of today's Yellow-eyed Penguins.

Q: From what flying birds did penguins evolve?

A: Despite all the modern morphological, genetic, and taxonomic analyses that have been thrown at this question, the answer remains elusive. In essence, representatives of three groups of modern flying birds share enough similarities with penguins to suggest that they could have had a common ancestor. These are: the petrels and albatrosses, the loons, and the frigatebirds.

Q: How many species of penguins are there alive today?

A: This, also, is not an easy question to answer definitively. Most authorities suggest between 16 to 18 species, but it all comes down to what you define as a species. Species are supposed to be non-interbreeding populations of animals. Yet, many authorities list the Royal Penguin, which breeds on Macquarie Island south of Australia, as a separate species even though it is likely that it is simply a white-faced variant of the much more widely dispersed Macaroni Penguin, and one with which it can surely interbreed. Similarly, a lesser number of authorities also list the White-flippered Penguin, found breeding on Banks Peninsula and nearby Motanau Island on New Zealand's

South Island, as a separate species
when the evidence is unequivo-
cal that it freely interbreeds
with other Little Penguins
and, like the Royal Penguin,
deserves to be recognized as a subspecies
only. On the other hand, variants
of Rockhopper Penguins currently listed
as subspecies—and, possibly, other
subspecies of Little Penguins—are likely
to be reproductively isolated and merit
an upgrade to full species status. So, until
further DNA, behavioral, and morphological studies provide evidence one way
or the other, the best that can be said is
that there are at least 16 confirmed
species of penguins alive today and
possibly as many as 18 or, even, 19.

Left: Waved Albatrosses
may share more with
penguins than just the
Galápagos Islands:
they may have a
common ancestor.

Below: Rather than a
distinct species, Royal
Penguins breeding on
Macquarie Island are
probably no more than
pale-faced versions of
the Macaroni Penguin.

Penguin Phylogeny

Q: **What are the relationships between modern penguins?**

A: The penguin species alive today represent a much-reduced sample of the diversity of penguins found in the fossil record over the last 60 million years. The modern forms of the penguin go back in the fossil record only about 3 million years. Hence, trying to deduce anything about the evolutionary origins of penguins from analyzing their current relationships is a bit like trying to understand the invention of the printing press by examining modern computers and word processors. We can, however, use the likes of molecular systematics (DNA), morphology, and behavior to inform us about the evolutionary relationships between the living forms of penguins. Biologists employ a double-barreled naming system for all animals and plants. We, for example, are *Homo sapiens*; an Adelie Penguin is *Pygoscelis adeliae*. The first part of the name is always capitalized and is known as the generic name, or genus. The second part of the name is always lowercased and is the specific name: the name, which in combination with the genus, identifies only that animal or plant, meaning, it shares its name with no other species. Species that are similar share the same generic name; in other words, they belong to the same genus. Chinstrap Penguins are *Pygoscelis antarctica*; Gentoo Penguins are *Pygoscelis papua*. Implicit in this naming convention is the notion that members of the same genus are more closely related (they share a more recent

Above right: Although its common name —Chinstrap Penguin— is an apt description of its distinctive markings, its scientific name (*Pygoscelis antarctica*) tells us about its ancestry.

Below right: Crested penguins, such as this Snares Penguin, all belong to the genus *Eudyptes* and have yellow or orange crests above their eyes.

common ancestor) than they are to members of other genera. The 16 species of living penguins fall into six distinct genera: *Pygoscelis*, *Aptenodytes* (Emperor and King penguins), *Eudyptes* (Rockhopper, Macaroni, Fiordland, Snares, and Erect-crested penguins), *Megadyptes* (Yellow-eyed Penguin), *Eudyptula* (Little Penguin), and *Spheniscus* (African, Magellanic, Humboldt, and Galápagos penguins). New techniques allow the genetic molecules in the DNA and RNA of penguins to be sequenced, while a method of numerical taxonomy (the classification of animals and plants), known as cladistics, sorts the sequences into the most parsimonious family tree of relationships it can, based upon the assumptions that: (a) more closely related species will have more of their sequences in common, and (b) evolution should not have to reinvent the wheel. To illustrate the latter, if we had three penguins, for example, two with crests and one without, to say that one of the crested species evolved from the noncrested species but the other did not, would require the independent evolution of crests in two separate groups of penguins. Logically, this seems much less likely (albeit not impossible) than a family tree where both crested penguins are descended from the same ancestral species. As it happens, penguins belonging to the genus *Eudyptes* all have crests and cladistic analyses show that they are, indeed, all closely related to one another and that they are most aligned to the genus *Megadyptes*, of which the Yellow-eyed Penguin is the only living representative. Meanwhile, the *Eudyptula* and *Spheniscus* genera share closer common ancestors than they do to other groups of penguins. There is some debate about whether *Aptenodytes* or *Pygoscelis* are the most ancient of the modern penguin lineages (in other words, which genus diverged from other living penguins first), but perhaps the most surprising thing is that the representatives of both these genera inhabit the Antarctic and the most southerly reaches of the world's oceans.

The Humboldt Penguin is a member of the genus *Spheniscus*. The *Spheniscus* are often called "banded penguins" because of the distinct bands of black and white feathers that mark them.

Origins

Q: Did penguins evolve in the Antarctic?

A: Almost certainly not. Just because the antecedents of Emperor Penguins and Adelie Penguins may have arisen longer ago than, say, Galápagos Penguins, it cannot really tell us anything about the conditions under which the ancestors of penguins switched from flying machines to swimming machines. The evolution of modern penguins has taken place over the last three million years, whereas penguins parked their wings and began swimming about the southern seas around 60 million years ago. Back in the days when penguins made their first appearance, Antarctica did not exist as we know it today. It had been part of a supercontinent called Gondwana and it was still connected to South America, relatively warm and covered in trees. The southern seas 50 to 60 million years ago, during a time geologists call the Late Paleocene/Early Eocene, were temperate to subtropical.

We cannot be sure where penguins first evolved, but if anywhere deserves that claim, it is probably New Zealand. New Zealand is truly the penguin capital of the world. New Zealand is not only home to the first and oldest penguin fossils, but also the most numerous. Even today, New Zealand has the highest diversity of penguins of anywhere in the world: 9 of the world's 16 species of penguins breed within New Zealand or its territories (including its subantarctic islands and the Ross Sea sector of Antarctica), and another 4 are frequent visitors to its shores. About 25 million years ago, South America separated from Antarctica, creating the circumpolar ocean current that is the Southern Ocean. This was accompanied by dramatic cooling of the Antarctic

Over the last 200 million years, continental drift has split the landmasses that used to make up Gondwana, tearing asunder South America, Antarctica, and Australia, and forming the Southern Ocean, which now circulates around Antarctica.

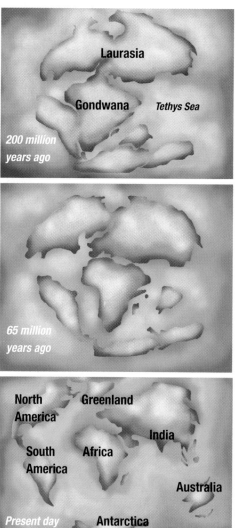

Laurasia

Gondwana   *Tethys Sea*

200 million years ago

65 million years ago

North America   Greenland

South America   Africa   India

Australia

Present day   Antarctica

continent. So, it was not that penguins evolved in cold climates such as the Antarctica we know now, it was that the adaptations they had developed to allow them to live a life in water—which acts as a huge heat sink for a warm-blooded animal—preadapted them to go where other birds feared to tread: to breed on the shores of the newly frozen (we are talking geological time here) continent, Antarctica.

Q: Were other seabirds becoming flightless, too?

A: Flightlessness is not unique to penguins. Among other waterbirds, however, it has evolved in only a small proportion of their members, such as the Flightless Galápagos Cormorant, the Flightless Steamerduck of South America, and its closely related neighbor, the Falkland Steamerduck. A couple of members of the duck family, the Auckland Island Teal and the Campbell Island Teal, evolved to be flightless in the very same areas that were hotbeds for penguin evolution. There were others, too, but they are now extinct. The feature that they all had in common was that flightlessness evolved in isolated areas, free of predators and where the birds had a supply of food close inshore that was available year-round. The scope for a flightless seabird seemed to be limited. It took penguins to seize the day and exploit the real opportunities that could be had by a diving bird that returned to the water.

Left: The Flightless Galápagos Cormorant could afford to go without wings because it has ample food close to shore and no predators.

Below: Home to a greater number of species than anywhere else, New Zealand is the penguin capital of the world. The oldest penguin fossils were found at Waipara, and the first fossils just north of Dunedin.

NEW ZEALAND

Auckland

NORTH ISLAND

Tasman Sea

Cook Strait

Wellington

Waipara

Pacific Ocean

SOUTH ISLAND

Christ Church

Dunedin

Foreaux Strait

Stewart Island

Snares Islands

RETURNING TO THE WATER

Life on Earth began in the sea: from some primordial soup more than 3.5 billion years ago to the evolution of fish some 3 billion years later. The fish then begat amphibians, which in turn begat reptiles, and, somewhere along the way, maybe 150 million years ago, the first birds appeared. Of the terrestrial vertebrates (land animals that have backbones as we do), some—for reasons known only to themselves—opted to return to an aquatic lifestyle. There were the plesiosaurs, the whales and dolphins, the seals, the sea turtles, and, of course, the penguins. Except that it is not so easy to turn back the evolutionary clock: evolution is progressive. Once fins have become legs, they cannot become fins again (legs could conceivably be modified into an approximation of fins, but beneath the superficial resemblance, there could be no disguising that they were still legs). The gills had gone. The scales had gone. Their teeth had gone. They had become warm-blooded. For penguins to become like fish again, they would have to emulate what it is to be a fish by modifying the very characteristics that make them birds.

Above: Snares Penguins do battle with the surf: probably not what they expected when they enrolled in Bird 101.

Left: A Magellanic Penguin "flies" underwater with wings modified to work like pectoral fins and feet that act as a rudder in the same way as a fish's tail.

Size Matters

Q: Why did penguins want to become like fish again?

A: At the time penguins evolved, the dinosaurs were already dead but the whales, dolphins, and seals were still but a twinkle in evolution's eye. The sea, then, represented a vast dinner plate of largely untapped resources for a diving seabird. Although there were seabirds to take advantage of those—the likes of the diving petrels, the cormorants, the gannets, and boobies—really, they only scratched the surface of the sea: much greater prizes awaited an animal that could dive down deep, really deep. But that was the catch-22 for birds. The very characteristics they needed to keep them aloft while flying (light weight and wide wing span) were the opposite of those needed to go down deep (a solid, dense body and short, stiff paddles). Advantages accrued to those with body designs that allowed them to dive deeper: they brought back more food, had more offspring, and those offspring helped proliferate those characteristics. Flying birds such as auks and puffins compromised their flying ability in order to dive deeper, having relatively short wings for the size of their bodies. But you cannot fight physics forever. As body mass increases, the surface area of wings needed to counter gravity and sustain flight increases, too. Large fragile wings are useless for propelling oneself through the much denser medium of water. At a certain weight, the size of wings needed to keep a body aloft become incompatible with diving. It seems that the cutoff is at about 2.2 pounds (1 kg).

Q: How big were the first penguins?

A: The first penguins were undoubtedly small, most likely with a body mass of about one kilogram. There are, of course, large flying seabirds, such as albatrosses, but they are not divers, as are penguins. Albatrosses' wings are too fragile and would break from the exertion needed to get their large but buoyant bodies down to any depth. It seems inconceivable, then, that the transition from a flying diver to a flightless diver took place anywhere but at that transition of approximately one-kilogram body mass. In order to dive deeper, penguins had to forsake flying in exchange for even larger body size. It is probably no coincidence that the smallest penguins, living and extinct, are and were, respectively, about one kilogram.

Atlantic Puffins dive to catch fish, but the need to fly limits their size and, ultimately, how deep they can dive.

Q: What is the world's smallest penguin?

A: The world's smallest penguin is the Little Penguin. It goes by various other names—Little Blue Penguin, Blue Penguin, and Fairy Penguin—and weighs not much more than 2.2 pounds (1 kg) soaking wet. It lives in Australia and New Zealand.

The world's smallest penguin answers, appropriately enough, to "Little Penguin." It is also called Little Blue Penguin for the distinct bluish tinge of its feathers.

Q: What is the world's largest penguin?

A: The Emperor Penguin is the undisputed super heavyweight champion of the world of penguins. Male Emperors can tip the scales at a whopping 84 pounds (38 kg), while females are relatively svelte, being a feather or two shy of 66 pounds (30 kg). Emperor Penguins live and breed in Antarctica.

Q: What is the largest penguin that has ever lived?

A: While physics constrained flying diving birds from being heavier than about one kilogram, once penguins gave up any pretense of flight, the shackles of such constraints disappeared and they were free to become as big as they liked. The largest penguin ever known from the fossil record was *Anthropornis nordenskjoeldi*. Although its name was a bit of a mouthful, at 5.8 feet tall (1.7 m) and more than 220 pounds (100 kg) in weight, it was probably safest to simply call it "sir." Not all penguins became so large; in fact, most penguins are in the order of 11 to 13 pounds (5–6 kg). Having got rid of the constraints for flying, they found themselves facing new ones: those that limit an object's ability to move through water efficiently. And, chief among them was resistance and the need for streamlining.

Humans generally consider "big" and "fat" to be undesirable adjectives, but these two characteristics allow the Emperor Penguin to breed in Antarctica during the frigid winter.

Body Shape

Above: Sea lions and penguins share the same spindle shape that allows them to move gracefully through water—although far less so on land.

Right: Built to move efficiently through water, on land, penguins look like upright torpedoes on feet.

Q: Why do penguins all have the same shape?

A: If penguins all look like they have been made from the same mold, it is not because of a lack of imagination on evolution's part. Put quite bluntly, other body designs just do not cut it when it comes to moving through water. Look about in the seas and you will see the same design repeated over and over: fish have it, whales have it, seals have it. It is a distinct spindle shape, with a pointed front, rounded sides, and a tapering tail; and when penguins took to the water, it was a fair bet that evolution would dictate that they should have it, too. The reason they have it is simple: no other shape is so streamlined and moves so efficiently through water. Underwater, animals with a spindle shape can move more quickly and yet consume less energy. There are, of course, variations on the spindle theme. Those that do not need to move quite so efficiently or quite so fast, such as reef fish, can afford to have a few embellishments or specifications outside the building code. But those that take to the open ocean, as do penguins, need to get the most miles per gallon they can.

Q: Just how efficient is the body shape of penguins?

A: Experiments in water and wind tunnels have demonstrated that the body shape of penguins is not just the most streamlined of any animal; it is more streamlined than any vehicle designed by humans. Coefficients of drag for penguins are the lowest recorded; lower than that for any car. So far so good: In their transition back to living like a fish, penguins had managed, then, to revert to a shape at least as good if not better than that of any fish. The penguins had another advantage too: they came turbo-charged.

Q: How does being warm-blooded help propel penguins?

A: Chemical reactions occur more quickly at higher temperatures. The fuel that drives a penguin is the same as that which drives us: fats, proteins, and sugars stored in the body or brought into it as food are ripped apart by a chain of chemical reactions, releasing the energy that makes muscles contract and an animal move. For every 10 degrees Celsius rise in temperature, the rate of these chemical reactions approximately doubles. By being warm-blooded, penguins can convert food and body reserves to energy much more efficiently than can a fish, providing the fuel for swimming and diving. But there is one huge potential downside to being a warm-blooded aquatic animal: hypothermia.

Penguin evolution had to solve how to remain warm-blooded in cold water. Although hypothermia is a threat, being warm-blooded means that penguins can convert food to energy more efficiently than can cold-blooded fish.

Penguins such as this Humboldt Penguin have the most streamlined shape of any animal; in fact, penguins are the most streamlined animals on Earth.

Feather Survival Suits

Q: **How do penguins stay warm in the water?**

A: Water conducts heat away from the body about 25 times faster than does air. Animals like ourselves, which must maintain a constant body temperature to survive, succumb to hypothermia (cooling of the body's core temperature) if we are immersed in water too long. In temperate waters, we could survive for a few hours; in Antarctic waters, we would last only minutes—yet penguins flourish in such conditions. Other warm-blooded animals that have returned to the sea, such as whales, dolphins, and seals, rely on a thick layer of blubber to insulate them. Penguins, on the other hand, while they have some fat, rely largely on their feathers. The feathers of a penguin make up its survival suit: they trap a layer of air next to the skin, insulating the bird in ways not dissimilar to the wet suit of a human diver. The feathers are such efficient insulators

that a lot of the heat generated by muscular activity while swimming is retained within the body. As a consequence, the undersides of the flippers of penguins that have just emerged from the water will often appear pink as they shunt blood near the surface to cool down when on land.

Q: **How are the feathers different on penguins from other birds?**

A: Pick up an abandoned gull's feather on a beach and you will notice its large size, its large surface area, and its light weight: all characteristics that help with flight. The feathers of flying birds such as gulls are also asymmetrical, with the stem of the vane separating a smaller side on the leading edge and a wider side on the trailing edge. The feathers also vary according to where they are on the bird, with the wing feathers, in particular, being different. Penguin feathers, by

From a King Penguin's perspective, the best thing about its feathers is not their striking coloration but that they keep it warm when splashing into icy Antarctic waters.

contrast, are symmetrical, short, and stiff. The feathers have hooks on them that lock together with the surrounding feathers, which are—with the exception of a few long tail feathers and very short feathers on the flippers—all roughly the same size, type, and shape. At their base are long downy filaments that fill the layer between the skin and outer parts of the feathers, cocooning the air like the filling of a duvet.

Q: How warm-blooded are penguins?

A: Penguins generate so much heat when swimming that sometimes when they come on land they need to dissipate that heat and, because the feathers on the flippers are shorter and provide less insulation, they engorge the capillaries there with blood, turning the undersides of their flippers pink. At other times, when the birds are cold, they shut down the capillaries feeding the surfaces of their flippers and feet. It is a sort of exaggerated cooling system that we all have. Get hot and our capillaries open and we turn red; get cold, they shut down and we turn pale. Where the penguins have gone one step further is to have a sophisticated countercurrent system. This works a bit like a heat pump that warms and cools a house. Essentially, blood from the surface is tracked alongside vessels bringing warm blood from the penguin's core, taking heat into one and cooling the other, all of which helps the penguins to maintain a constant core temperature.

Penguins keep their body temperature a few degrees above our own, at about 102°F (39°C). It is one thing to be warm-blooded, to have the same body shape, and the same feathers, but none of that explains why penguins should all have more or less the same paint job.

Areas where the skin is exposed, such as the feet of this Magellanic Penguin, can be used to control body temperature by adjusting the blood flow to them.

Just out of water, the undersides of a penguin's flippers will often appear pink as the bird shunts blood to them to rid itself of excess body heat.

> They are extraordinarily like children, these little people of the Antarctic world, either like children, or like old men, full of their own importance and late for dinner, in their black tail-coats and white shirt-fronts—and rather portly withal.
>
> —APSLEY CHERRY-GARRARD, BRITISH EXPLORER OF THE ANTARCTIC

Penguin Colors

Q: Why do penguins look like they are wearing tuxedos?

A: All penguins conform pretty much to the same dress code. Their color scheme is notable for its lack of color,

A male isabelline Adelie Penguin performs an ecstatic display in a bid to attract a mate.

with white bellies and dark, usually black, backs the fashion de rigueur on penguin-walks all over the Southern Hemisphere. In fact, it is not something peculiar to them. Look at the killer whale, the shark, the tuna—all hunters in the open ocean. In the sea, there is nowhere for predators like them to hide. They cannot sneak through long grass. They cannot crouch behind bushes. Their color scheme is their camouflage. Light bellies blend in with the surface when seen from below; dark backs merge with the murky depths when seen from above. The pigment that makes the feathers black is called mela-nin. But not all penguins are black.

Q: Why are Little Penguins blue?

A: Little Penguins have bellies that are white, but the plumage on their backs has a bluish tinge. In essence, there are different types of melanin and the color that is reflected by the feathers depends upon the type and concentration of melanin deposited in the feathers by melanin-producing cells at the base of the feathers. The slate blue produced by their feathers is surely why Little Penguins are often called Little Blue Penguins or, even, just Blue Penguins.

Q: Are there albino penguins?

A: True albinism—a pure white bird that produces no melanin to color its feathers—is exceedingly rare in penguins, but it does occur. In many penguin species, however, there is a genetic muta-tion that occurs much more frequently (perhaps one in every 100 thousand birds) and which causes the feathers on the back to be blonde rather than black. Birds with this condition are known as isabellines, and it seems that they have very low levels of melanin. Penguin biologists have long been interested not so much in whether blondes have more fun, but whether they have any fun at all. It turns out that isabelline birds breed normally, raising issues about what exactly it is that penguins use to determine a suitable mate.

Q: Are the colored bits of penguins for mating?

A: Although the world of penguins is largely black and white, several species have notable splotches of color. The Emperor and King penguins have yellow to orange cheek patches and colored fleshy pads on their bills; all five species of crested penguins (those belonging to the genus *Eudyptes*) have yellow crests of one sort or another sticking out above their eyes like eyebrows on steroids; Yellow-eyed Penguins have not only yellow eyes but also a band of yellow feathers that runs through the eyes and around the back of their heads. Even those penguins eschewing color have distinct markings: the white eye ring of the Adelie; the cap of white feathers on the Gentoo; the thin black band that gives the Chinstrap its name; the various bands of black feathers on the faces and chests of penguins belonging to the genus *Spheniscus* (which is why they are sometimes known as the banded or ringed penguins). It seems that all these accoutrements, colored or not, basically function in the same way: they are markers to the birds that identify their species, a source of potential mates. In the language of the scientist, they are for species recognition. In practice, that means simply that it is the first thing a penguin should look for when choosing a mate, otherwise it might be wasting its time. Of course, it needs to be old enough first.

Q: How does the plumage of juveniles differ from that of adults?

A: In many species of penguins, juveniles have a slightly different plumage from that of adults. For example, adolescent Adelie Penguins have a white chin, rather than the black chin of adults. By the time they become reproductively active, they will have molted into the full adult plumage. Young *Spheniscus* penguins lack the bands of their parents and, in so doing, look remarkably like the adults of Little Penguins. It is not always clear why juvenile birds should have different markings but one oft-given reason is that it marks them out as not posing a threat to breeding adults and, therefore, reduces the likelihood that they will get a flipper-bashing for their troubles.

A bad hair day? Its shocking yellow crest may appear unruly, but it is what makes a Rockhopper Penguin attractive to another Rockhopper Penguin.

King Penguins eschew feather crests in favor of delicately shaded orange highlights. Juvenile Kings sport a coat of drab brown feathers that make them easily distinguishable as nonbreeders.

Flippers and Feet

Q: Why are the flippers of penguins so stiff?

A: The wings of penguins have been modified from those requirements for flying in air to those needed for flying underwater. They are thin, stiff, and tapered. The buoyancy of water means that they are required not so much to maintain uplift against gravity, but to propel the animal forward. To that end, they must be streamlined. Like a plane's wing they are thicker at the front edge and tapered to a thin edge on the trailing edge, thereby reducing turbulence. Although a penguin's flipper can be folded in a horizontal plane at the elbow, much of the flexibility of a flying bird's wing has been lost in favor of becoming a powerful paddle that really only moves where the wing joins the body. The feathers on the flippers are also much reduced in size, further reducing drag. Because any protrusion sticking outside the spindle shape of the penguin's body will create drag, natural selection arrived quickly at the optimum size and shape for penguin flippers. Flipper size and shape does not vary much between different penguin species other than to scale with body size (in other words, larger penguins have larger flippers in proportion to their increased size). In contrast, other aspects of a penguin's anatomy, such as bill size

The thin, stiff, tapered flippers of penguins are really wings that have been modified to function as paddles.

and shape, can be much more variable because they have less impact on drag. Given that the mantra of just about all aspects of penguin design is to maximize streamlining and minimize drag, that will, of course, apply to protrusions such as feet as well.

Q: Why are penguins' feet so far back?

A: The feet of penguins, unlike underwater diving birds such as cormorants, are not used for propulsion. As such, legs and feet represent protrusions that will contribute to drag and slow the animal down, not make it go faster. The penguins' solution—or rather, the solution evolution has foisted on them—is to reduce the size of the legs and move them to the very back of their spindle-shaped bodies, where they function as a rudder when swimming underwater. By sticking their feet out at a particular angle, penguins can control the direction in which they travel, similar to using a tiller to control the angle of the rudder on a small boat. One consequence of deriving a body plan that enhances performance in one world, the aquatic one, however, is that it can lead to compromises in another.

Q: Why do penguins walk funny?

A: Short little legs pushed to the back end of the body work well when it comes to reducing drag underwater, but make walking on land awkward, if not downright difficult at times. The stance of penguins

is much more upright than it is in other birds, with a back that appears more or less straight and perpendicular to the ground. Although all birds are bipedal—that is, they walk on two legs as we do—it is the upright stance of penguins, with their shortened gait from their short little legs, that makes them look faintly human; albeit humans with a better dress sense

than most of us. It also means that balance can be more of a problem for a penguin moving about on land than it is for other birds. Television documentaries are fond of playing this up, setting the slipping, sliding, and falling over that often accompanies walking penguins to music that lends it an air of slapstick. That really does penguins a disservice, however; for while, in order to maximize their underwater efficiency, there are undoubted compromises to the way they walk, penguins manage remarkably well in a terrestrial environment. In many places penguins clamber up terrifyingly steep cliffs to reach their nesting sites. Rockhopper Penguins, especially, deserve praise as befits their name. Watch Rockhopper Penguins scale a 600-foot near-vertical cliff, as do those breeding on Sea Lion Island in the Falkland Islands, and you will not laugh if you see one fall over. They are not slapstick funny in the way they walk; they are Clint Eastwood tough.

Co-opting feet as rudders in the water meant that on land penguins had little choice but to stand upright as does this African Penguin.

"Make my day": Chinstrap Penguins walk tough. Although popular culture images of penguins play up the comical aspect of their awkward gait on land, penguins are remarkably adapted to their harsh environments.

Penguin Bones

Q: What is the tarsometatarsus?

A: If Clint Eastwood could be one bone in a penguin's body, he would undoubtedly be the tarsometatarsus (the fused anklebone that supports the penguin when walking): it is tougher than any other and seems to last forever. The most obvious characteristic of the tarsometatarsus is that it is short; the appendages of the flying bird have been reduced as much as is practicable to decrease drag when swimming, although still providing support when on land. Walking upright on such stubby legs, which have been placed at the very back of their bodies, is what gives penguins their waddling gait, like kids trying to walk in a sack. The tarsometatarsus is the most commonly preserved bone found by penguin fossil hunters. They are distinctive and diagnostic of penguins, which is

fortunate, because often the tarsometatarsus is the only bone that is preserved. Another bone that is often fossilized is the humerus (the wing bone that joins the body; in us it is the bone in our upper arm), and, like the tarsometatarsus and all the other bones in a penguin's body, the humerus is very dense.

Q: Why are penguin bones so heavy?

A: Pick up a penguin bone, say the humerus, and the equivalent bone from a flying bird. Drop both bones into some water and you will see a difference: the bone from the flying bird will float; the one from the penguin will sink. One of the most amazing adaptations of birds when they first took to the air was the advent of hollow bones. Stretched throughout a bird's hollow bones are outgrowths of the lungs that are filled with air. A flying bird's bones have struts, making them both strong and light. The feathers of a frigatebird, for example, weigh more than its skeleton. As any duck shooter and Labrador retriever knows, kill a bird such as a duck and it will float—its specific gravity is less than that of water. All of which is great news for flying but anathema for diving. Human divers strap on weight belts to make them sink and counteract their buoyancy. The alternative evolution came up with for penguins was to make their bones more solid, making a penguin a lot heavier than a similar-sized flying bird. It sounds like something a tire manufacturer might say, but penguin bones are described as nonpneumatic,

T. H. Huxley's original illustration of the metatarsal bone of *Palaeeudyptes antarcticus,* the first penguin fossil ever discovered.

672   PROCEEDINGS OF THE GEOLOGICAL SOCIETY.   [March 23,

Fig. 1.—*Front view of the right tarso-metatarse of* Palæeudyptes antarcticus. Nat. size.

Fig. 2.—*Back view of the same bone* (fig. 1.). Nat. size.

Built for efficiency in water, penguins such as these Adelies have dense bones that aid diving but not flying.

Unlike a penguin, most birds have light, "pneumatic" bones. Air-filled spaces are apparent in a cross-section of a flying bird's bone.

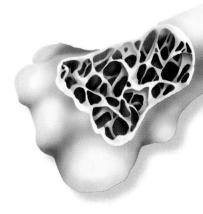

to distinguish them from the pneumatic or air-filled bones of most other birds. Interestingly, the only other family of entirely flightless birds, the ratites—which include the Ostrich, Rhea, and extinct Moa—also have nonpneumatic bones. Although they are not waterbirds, their bones must support huge body sizes; so in their case, their more solid bones are for strength rather than to make them sink. All these structural changes that took a flying bird and modified it into something more like a torpedo were the necessary consequences of some precursor penguin choosing to run away—well, waddle away—to a life at sea.

CHAPTER 3

LIFE AT SEA

Penguins, more than any other birds, deserve to be called "seabirds." They spend most of their lives at sea: perhaps 80 percent or more. As far as possible, they have again become aquatic like their fishy ancestors. There is no "undo button" for evolution, however; they cannot just shake off their immediate past in favor of their distant past. There are things that prevent them from reverting completely to fish. Penguins are air breathers and must remain so. They can stay underwater only for as long as they can hold their breaths. But, more than anything, it is their system of reproduction that means they will be forever tied to the land: they lay porous eggs, designed to let oxygen in and carbon dioxide out, and, most important, the eggs contain warm-blooded embryos that must be incubated to keep them warm. The internal gestation of whales and dolphins, another group of land vertebrates that returned to the water, meant that they could live in the aquatic world completely. But their eggs—the very things that mark them out as birds—mean that penguins must live in two worlds. Compromise, then, is the price penguins must pay to go back to the sea.

Above: Eggs that must be incubated, one of the hallmarks of birds, tie the otherwise aquatic penguin to the land.

Left: It may have been the air that called to their ancestors, but it is the sea that calls to penguins.

Food Glorious Food

Q: What is it that penguins eat that makes going back to the sea so attractive to them?

A: Penguins, in becoming like fish again, are really the high-octane fishlike equivalents of super cars: They have become super fish. And just like a Lamborghini, they are expensive to run. To power the costs of swimming through water, of diving, of staying warm, and, especially, to accommodate a lifestyle where they must often remove themselves from their food supply and alternate long periods of fasting between the feasting, they must have access to a highly concentrated food supply. To that end, penguins forage primarily on schooling prey that occur in clumps within the three-dimensional ocean: small fish, krill, and squid.

Penguins living in tropical to temperate zones tend to feed mainly on fish. In the Antarctic—where summer's 24-hour daylight leads to huge phytoplankton (the plants of the sea) blooms, which in turn feed great stocks of zooplankton—penguins can feed almost exclusively on krill (shrimplike crustaceans that are by far and away the most important constituents of the zooplankton in southern waters). At latitudes in between, penguins tend to take a mixture of fish, krill, and squid.

Summer in Antarctica, when the sea ice has broken up, is a time of plenty for the likes of Adelie Penguins.

in the south (where the die-off of phytoplankton and zooplankton that occurs after each summer's massive blooms provides detritus that breaks down and fills the water with nutrients), and this upwells and fertilizes the waters around the Galápagos and on the coasts of Peru and Chile, creating oases of high productivity that Galápagos, Humboldt, and Magellanic penguins have come to rely upon.

Although we may be familiar with the great variety of fish that tropical reefs host, the seas around them are relatively empty, depauperate of life. Penguins evolved in the Southern Hemisphere because the lack of predators enabled them to give up flight, but it is probably the low productivity of tropical seas that keeps them locked below the equator. It is why there are no penguins in Tahiti or Fiji: they have no nutrients delivered to their doors by the underwater highways that are the world's ocean currents. And it is why there are no penguins in California or Hawaii: there simply are not enough fueling stations for penguins to power their energy-expensive bodies through the aquatic equivalent of deserts that are tropical seas.

Pinnacle Rock, Isla Bartolome, home to a population of Galápagos Penguins. The Galápagos Islands are the northernmost outpost of penguindom.

Magellanic Penguins —indeed, all of the banded penguins— rely on nutrients brought by cold currents from the south to fertilize the seas where they feed.

Q: If penguins can find food in the tropics, why have they not moved into the Northern Hemisphere?

A: In fact, penguins really only live in warm areas such as the tropics where cold currents from the far south deliver nutrients to those waters, thereby creating a food supply concentrated enough to fuel the penguins' expensive energetic needs. The Benguela Current carries the nutrients to South Africa and Namibia that ultimately sustain the anchovies and pilchards on which the African Penguins feed; the Leeuwin Current takes similarly cold nutrient-rich waters to the western side of Australia, fueling Little Penguins; and the Humboldt Current travels up the western side of South America before taking a detour from Peru out to the Galápagos Islands, which sit, mostly, just a smidgen below the equator. As with the others, the Humboldt Current transports nutrients from the cold but superproductive seas

Accessing Food

The hook on the tip of the Humboldt's bill can be used to grasp its prey.

The bills of banded penguins, such as this Humboldt, reveal that they are primarily fish-eaters.

Q: Why do some penguins have hooked bills?

A: Banded penguins, those belonging to the genus *Spheniscus,* live closest to the equator. One characteristic that sets them apart from many penguins, as any penguin researcher who has ever handled them can tell you, is that they have extremely sharp bills with a hook at the end of the top mandible that can slice a researcher's arm as easily as a knife. It is a characteristic that they share with the crested penguins, which feed primarily on fish and squid. These hooks are actually adaptations that enable the penguins to catch a fish more easily (perhaps it is fortunate that hydrodynamics limit the size of a penguin's flippers, or we could only imagine the stories they might tell about the ones that got away).

Q: What is so special about krill?

A: Penguins feeding almost exclusively on krill, such as the Adelie and Chinstrap penguins, have bills without hooks. In their case, the food items are small enough that they are swallowed, not held, with a penguin catching maybe a score or more on a single dive. Krill may be small but they occur in dense clumps: the biomass of krill in Antarctic waters is greater than that for any other animal on the planet.

It would be wrong, however, to think of penguins as fussy eaters specialized to feed exclusively on one particular prey type. Essentially, they are opportunistic feeders and will take whatever suitable food is available. For example, although a single species of krill, *Euphausia superba,* makes up more than 98 percent of the diet of Adelie Penguins breeding around the Antarctic Peninsula, those on the other side of Antarctica, in the Ross Sea, opt for a more varied diet, mixing Antarctic silverfish with two types of krill.

The main thing is that the individually small food items that penguins eat need to be concentrated into clumps to make it worth their while (that is, for the energy gained to exceed the energy expended on fishing effort). The trick for penguins, then, is to locate these rewarding clumps in three-dimensional space.

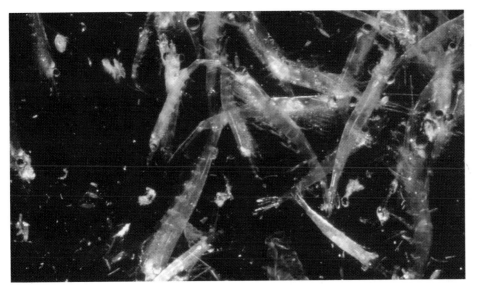

Krill are the rice of the Antarctic ecosystem, the staple food in the diets of so many of the animals that live there, including penguins.

Q: **How far do penguins travel at sea to get food?**

A: Flying seabirds such as albatross and petrels can cover large distances quickly, which means that their food supply can often be at great distances from their breeding sites. Put another way, they are not so limited in where they can choose to breed by where their food is located. Swimming through water is not only expensive energetically, in terms of miles traveled per unit of energy consumed, it is also costly in terms of time. Take too long to get food and you risk your mate deserting the nest or your chicks starving.

It turns out that the distance that penguins travel to get food is highly variable. Some species, such as African, Gentoo, and Yellow-eyed penguins, normally travel only a few miles from shore to find their meals, whereas King Penguins can travel a thousand miles or more at certain times of the breeding cycle. Other species, such as

Adelie, Macaroni, and Snares penguins measure distances in tens of miles, sometimes even hundreds. Distance traveled can even vary within species, depending upon where the breeding site is relative to the feeding sites.

African Penguins like to feed close to the shore, usually only a few miles from their nesting sites.

Monitoring Penguins at Sea

Q: **How do we know how far penguins travel at sea?**

A: Although penguins have always been more waterbird than land bird, our knowledge of them until fairly recently

Satellite telemetry has been used to track Emperor Penguins through pack-ice and the harshest Antarctic conditions, which would be impossible to do otherwise.

was based largely upon their on-land antics—the breeding side of their lives—because that was all we could see. The miniaturization of electronics that has occurred from the 1970s onward, however, has allowed us to use telemetry to monitor the behavior of penguins at sea. Electronic devices are attached to penguins that are small enough for them to carry but powerful enough to send a signal to receiving towers (radiotelemetry) or satellites (satellite telemetry). More recently, data loggers with onboard computer chips have

been used to store GPS (global positioning system) locations from satellites, providing an accuracy no longer measured in miles but in meters. Data loggers can also be used to store information on depth (pressure), speed, temperature, salinity, light, or whether the device is wet or not (which indicates whether the penguin is in or out of water).

From the data sent to satellites or downloaded to computers, we can reconstruct the trips penguins take at sea. We know where they go, how they traveled there, and what they did once they got there. We can even tell when they have been eating, with devices that measure temperature in the stomach (temperature drops when penguins swallow food and cold water) or the gape of the bill (penguins open wide to take in their prey).

Q: **What happens when a radio-telemetry device is attached to the streamlined body of a penguin?**

A: Streamlining is especially important for penguins, so any device that is attached to them is likely to have some energetic consequences. Early devices used to study their at-sea behavior were big, heavy, and had large cross-sectional areas. The latter is especially crucial as the bigger the area, the more resistance (in other words, thick attachments increase drag). Penguins do show a remarkable capacity to adjust to extra drag, but the question remains as to whether their subsequent behavior recorded by the devices represents normal behavior. By placing devices near the tail of the penguin and shaping them like a Formula One car, with a tapered nose so as to reduce their cross-sectional area, the amount of drag can be minimized and, with it, any effects on behavior.

Q: Is it possible for penguins to map the oceans for us?

A: Data loggers that can accurately plot location and depth in combination with such variables as salinity and temperature can potentially be used to tell us not just about the penguins but also the oceans in which they live. Scientists have come to realize, therefore, that in trying to uncover the at-sea lives of penguins, they are also able to use the penguins as relatively inexpensive unpaid workers to map the conditions of the seas in which they live. Of course, the area monitored is limited by how far the penguins go.

Left: To minimize drag, attachments to penguins should be streamlined and placed low on the back.

Below: Penguins travel extensively through the three-dimensional space that is the sea; potentially, we can harness them to collect data there.

"These guys are so cute, and that's what attracts us to them. But they're also very sophisticated animals, perfectly adapted to their environment."

—GREG WHITTAKER, ANIMAL-HUSBANDRY CURATOR

Inshore versus Offshore Feeding

Above: King Penguins are the offshore swimming champions, traveling farther to get food than any other penguin species.

Below: Proving that it does not just run in the family, Gentoo Penguins are inshore feeders, although their cousins the Adelie and Chinstrap penguins are offshore feeders.

Q: **How do penguins differ in their feeding patterns?**

A: It is possible to categorize penguins into two broad categories based on how far they travel to get food: inshore feeders and offshore feeders. Inshore feeders tend to inhabit lower latitudes and feed on fish available year-round. They make short, frequent trips to sea, usually feeding well within 12.5 miles (20 km) of the shore and colony. In contrast, offshore feeders travel tens and sometimes hundreds of miles to get food, especially during the incubation period. They tend to occur at higher latitudes where food supply is more seasonal and, as a consequence, they migrate away from the nesting areas during the nonbreeding period. Even when feeding chicks, which limits how far the parents can go because their chicks must be fed regularly, offshore feeders tend to travel farther than do inshore-feeding species. The following are normally regarded as inshore feeders:

African, Galápagos, Gentoo, Humboldt, Little, and Yellow-eyed penguins. Offshore feeders consist of Adelie, Chinstrap, Emperor, King, Magellanic, and all the crested species (Erect-crested, Fiordland, Macaroni, Rockhopper, and Snares).

Q: **How long do penguins stay away from the nest to feed?**

A: The eggs and young chicks of all of the penguin species must be guarded and brooded at all times to protect them from predators and from becoming cold. This means that one partner must remain on the nest while the other is at sea obtaining food. In inshore-feeding penguins, parents tend to swap attendance on the nest every day or so. In contrast, offshore-feeding penguins tend to be away from the nests for many days, if not weeks at a time, while the eggs are being incubated (they cannot afford to be away for so long once their chicks hatch).

In contrast to the residential inshore-feeding penguins in warmer climes, penguins in the colder south are exposed to a food supply that tends to be highly seasonal with exceptional peaks of productivity, especially at oceanic fronts where different bodies of water meet. The Antarctic Circumpolar Current, that part of the Southern Ocean that circles continuously in an eastward direction around the Antarctic continent, is associated with a polar front on its southern side and a subantarctic front on its northern edge. These fronts are typically

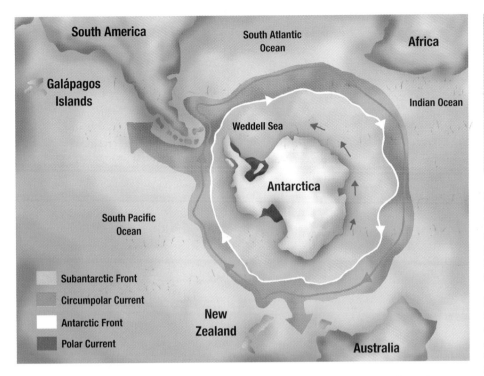

- **Subantarctic Front**
- **Circumpolar Current**
- **Antarctic Front**
- **Polar Current**

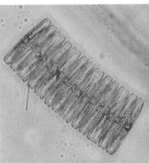

Above: A greatly magnified view of phytoplankton. These minuscule plants of the sea undergo a population explosion in response to nutrients and the summer sun.

Left: The Circumpolar Current takes water clockwise around Antarctica. Fronts occur where different bodies of water meet.

Below: Snares Penguins feed at the Subtropical Front, some 100 miles from where they breed.

areas in which there is turbulence and upwelling—where nutrients are brought to the surface, fertilizing blooms of plankton that flourish in the long summer days. Such areas of high productivity are extremely attractive to penguins, but they often occur at great distances from the nearest available nesting sites. Offshore foraging penguins have evolved to capitalize on these distant bounties by staying at sea for up to two or three weeks while their mate remains on land sitting on the eggs.

For example, satellite telemetry has shown researchers that a subspecies of Macaroni Penguin, sometimes called the Royal Penguin, travel up to 400 miles (640 km) to feed at the polar front south of their homes on Macquarie Island. Similarly, GPS loggers used on Snares Penguins, which breed only on a small group of islands south of New Zealand

that go by the same name, show that male Snares penguins travel more than 100 miles (160 km) to get to another oceanic front, the Subtropical Front.

Feeding and Life History Patterns

Q: How does feeding distance affect penguins?

A: As trifling and prosaic as it may seem, feeding distance is probably the most crucial aspect affecting a penguin's way of life. Feeding distance affects just about everything that a penguin does. It is easier to illustrate this with examples.

Yellow-eyed Penguins breed primarily in the forests and vegetation on the southeastern coast of New Zealand's South Island and on the subantarctic Auckland Islands and Campbell Island. They feed mainly on bottom-dwelling fish that inhabit shallow nearby shelf waters year-round. This permits the penguins to pretty much remain resident on their breeding sites. They nest beneath vegetation, with their nests often quite distant from their neighbors. During incubation they swap nest duty with their partners every day or two and, once the chicks hatch, they swap every day. At every nest relief they engage in behavioral ceremonies that serve to reinforce their pair-bond. Couple that with the fact that they stay together and do not migrate and you have a recipe for a long and happy penguin marriage. Yellow-eyed Penguins have extremely high levels of mate fidelity.

In contrast, Adelie Penguins breeding in the Antarctic have a very narrow window in which food and conditions are favorable for breeding. During the eight months when conditions are not conducive to breeding, they migrate, and partners spend the winter months apart, feeding among the pack-ice. When they return to the colony at the start of the breeding season, there is precious little time to waste if their partner is not there. Nest reliefs occur only once every two to three weeks during incubation (because they go so far to get their food), so the pair-bond gets precious little reinforcement. Combine an urgency to breed (because feeding conditions will not last), with a lack of attention and long periods apart, and it is perhaps not surprising that divorce and relationship breakups are common in Adelie Penguins.

Q: Are feeding patterns hard-wired?

A: Although a penguin's feeding and breeding regimen can often appear consistent across a species, that is partly a reflection of the common ecological conditions in which they typically choose to breed. Were events to alter those conditions or some birds to breed in alternative conditions, we find that

Adelie Penguins are migratory and have a small window when conditions are conducive to breed in Antarctica; therefore Adelies are likely to change partners every breeding season.

penguins can respond by being quite plastic in their behavior. For instance, Little Penguins are usually described as inshore feeders, engaging in frequent nest reliefs, but in the Marlborough Sounds of New Zealand they adopt an offshore-feeding strategy in response to a more distant food supply. In contrast, the normally offshore-feeding Chinstrap Penguins will forage inshore in situations where they have an adequate food supply close to their colony.

Magellanic Penguins, breeding within a waddle of each other at the bottom of South America, spend longer periods at sea and have fewer nest reliefs at the site where they must travel farther and dive deeper to get food. Humboldt Penguins, breeding on the edge of Chile's Atacama Desert, normally forage close to shore and are nonmigratory, but, when El Niño conditions devastate their food supply, they switch to a far-ranging offshore strategy. It is all a matter of where the food is and how long it takes to get it.

The feeding strategies of Magellanic Penguins are influenced by their food supply.

Little Penguins are perhaps the most plastic of all the penguins in their feeding behavior, adopting an inshore- or offshore-feeding strategy depending upon conditions.

Porpoising and Predators

Q: How fast do penguins swim?

A: When traveling at sea, most penguins swim at around 6.5 feet (2 m) per second. The smallest penguins, Little Penguins, move a bit slower than this; the largest, Emperor Penguins, move a bit faster. When traveling to and from their feeding areas like this, they tend to remain near the surface and keep to a constant heading. Traveling faster than two meters per second costs penguins much more energy, which can reach a point where they forsake underwater swimming and fly, ever so briefly.

Above: Because of the high energetic costs to maintain the necessary speed, the large King Penguins rarely porpoise.

Below: The smaller penguins, such as these Snares, porpoise when they need to travel quickly.

Q: Why do penguins porpoise?

A: As the speed of penguins underwater increases, the amount of hydrodynamic drag increases exponentially. Put another way, the amount that the water resists the penguin moving through it increases. At a certain speed, the energetic costs become so high that it actually pays the penguin to leap clear of the water. That is, if the penguin wishes to go faster, it will cost it less energy if it spends some time moving through air, which is a lot easier to move through than is water. When penguins do this, we call it porpoising, after the similar mode of travel employed by dolphins and porpoises. For most penguins, the threshold when it pays them to porpoise occurs when they have their engines cranked up to about 10 feet (3 m) per second. It is not just that the air has less resistance, either; it is also an opportunity for them to catch a breath without slowing down when moving quickly. The speed at which it pays a penguin to porpoise increases with its body size, so that the largest penguins, the King and Emperor penguins, either seldom or never porpoise, respectively, because the energy needed to sustain speeds as high as four meters per second would hardly make traveling like that worthwhile for them.

Penguins sometimes use porpoising to travel quickly to a food source. Most evidently, however, penguins use porpoising as an escape response to flee from dangers such as predators.

than one might suppose. Sharks probably do not bother with them much, although they will take the odd foot left dangling in the water by a penguin sleeping on the surface. Killer whales certainly target the large King and Emperor penguins, but do not appear to trouble themselves with the smaller varieties, although there has been the odd rare sighting of one of them taking an Adelie Penguin.

Seals are probably an adult penguin's deadliest foe and, in particular, leopard seals. Although less likely to be able to take a penguin in open water, leopard seals are adept at waiting by the margins between the water and the land, intent on grabbing penguins as they get in or out. They frequently catch a panicked penguin that makes a mistake exiting the water and falls back in. They have also learned to hide in the murk where the silt-laden water of streams is flushed into the sea, and catch unsuspecting penguins that way. Other seals, especially sea lions, can also make a meal of penguins in certain locations. Even the odd Weddell seal in Antarctic waters has learned that Adelie Penguins can provide a bit of variety to a fish diet.

Although statistically the chances of a penguin being preyed upon are slight, that does not stop penguins appearing to fear entering the watery world they gave up flying to exploit.

Left: Although they have few natural predators, adult Adelie Penguins are most vulnerable to predators at the interface between water and land.

Below: A penguin's worst friend: The leopard seal's bite is worse than its bark. Leopard seals are known to lurk in the muddy margins where land and sea meet, watching to snag an unlucky penguin.

Q: **What predators do penguins face in the sea?**

A: Penguins may appear awkward on land, but underwater they are acrobats, capable of ducking and diving, spinning and turning, all at high speed. This makes them less vulnerable to predators

Diving

Q: **Before diving in, do penguins push each other in to test the waters?**

A: There is a popular misconception that penguins congregate at the water's edge and then push one of their number in to see whether it is safe and, if the bird is not eaten, the others will follow. As good a story as it makes, it is simply not true. It may well look like that from afar: penguins do often congregate on the shore and do seem to hesitate before jumping in. They do not, however, push each other in. They may jostle. And indeed, what often happens is that one or two may dive in and the rest hold back. At a certain point, with the mob mentality that they share with football fans, they will all surge forward and dive in. But that is not sacrifice; that is penguins behaving like sheep.

Q: **How does a penguin dive?**

A: Diving behavior of penguins can be described in detail from data loggers attached to penguins. The dives can be deep with very little bottom time (V dives) or they can have a flat bottom phase to them, when most likely the penguin is feeding (U dives). V dives are used primarily for searching for clumps of food. Once it has been found, the penguins make repeated dives to similar depths to feed on the food source.

Q: **How deep do penguins dive?**

A: All penguins are capable of diving to great depths. Maximum depth is a function of body size, which is why they had to give up flying, after all. With the possible exception of the smallest penguin, the Little Penguin, all penguins are capable of diving to depths over 328 feet (100 m). The largest, the Emperor Penguin can dive to over 1,650 feet (500 m). What is perhaps more remarkable is that they can dive down to these depths repeatedly. When feeding, for example, the relatively small (at 8.8 pounds, or 4 kg), Snares Penguins have been found to dive repeatedly, for hours at a time, to depths of around 425 feet (130 m). They take about three minutes on each dive. Emperor Penguins can take as long as

Although it may look like penguins push one of their colony-mates into the water to test its safety, there is no such thing as sacrificial lambs in the penguin world, just sheep.

accurately onto ice to avoid predators on the other. Remarkably, the penguin's eyes, which are similar to those of humans, are able to accommodate these perceptual changes through modifications to the cornea and retina, allowing them to see equally well above and below the waterline.

Penguins have evolved to be divers. Even Little Penguins can dive to 220 feet (67 m), and larger penguins are capable of plunging much deeper.

Q: **Do penguins travel in groups while at sea?**

A: One of the things that characterizes penguins is that they are gregarious, meaning that they like to hang out together; but they are unsociably so, meaning that they act independently of each other. Species such as the Little Penguin tend to go feeding on their own. Others, such as Adelies, stick within groups even when in the water. But at some point they all have to come out of the water, and that is when they really want to cluster in a group.

nine minutes. Despite their maximum dive capabilities, however, most penguins feed regularly within the top 230 feet (70 m) of the water column. This is because they are visual predators, which means that, unlike dolphins that use sonar to locate prey, penguins must be able to see their prey to catch it. Penguins that feed in the dark at great depths, such as the King and Emperor penguins, prey on bioluminescent species of squid and fish.

Q: **How do penguins judge distances in the water and out of it?**

A: If you have ever put on a mask and snorkeled, you will know that your perception of size and distances changes underwater. Things that look like goldfish from above the water become like monster sharks under it . . . well, that is an exaggeration, but they do look significantly bigger. And that is a potential problem for a bird that lives in two worlds and relies upon fine judgments of distances to catch food underwater on one hand, and to be able to leap

Penguins are social birds, with some species acting more independent than others. Certain penguins, such as these Adelies in Antarctica, like to stick together in and out of the water.

CHAPTER 4

FINDING A PLACE TO BREED

Penguins can spend as long as they like at sea, pretending to be fish or otherwise. They can be the sea's most successful hunter. But ultimately it will not matter a jot unless they can successfully breed. And that is where the penguin's chickenlike ancestors come home to roost so to speak: penguins must lay their eggs on land. This severely limits where a flightless bird dressed up in a feather cloak can breed.

If getting too cold is the threat that a warm-blooded bird must overcome to live in the sea, getting too hot is the risk such a bird faces when it comes ashore unable to dress to chill. Penguins must wear the same wardrobe whatever the weather. Being flightless leaves penguins vulnerable to those that find them attractive as food. Any breeding site should provide protection from predators, in addition to offering protection from the elements. It must also be close enough to the coast that the penguins can walk to it readily. And, of course, penguins can only consider sites that are close enough to their food supply that they can swim to it while incubating and rearing chicks. In short, the perfect place for a penguin to live on land can be very hard to find.

Above: African Penguins have a penchant for making their homes on some of the finest beaches in South Africa.

Left: Snares Penguins do not like it hot, nesting in the shade of forest clearings in their subantarctic habitat.

Nesting with Latitude

Contradicting the misconception that penguins are creatures of the cold, Humboldt Penguins nest next to cacti in the deserts of northern Chile and Peru.

Q: If penguins are birds, does that mean that they nest in trees?

A: Penguins nest in a variety of places: within the cracks of old lava floes on the Galápagos Islands; burrowed into the guano of pelicans in Peru; next to cactus in the deserts of Chile; in caves on New Zealand's Banks Peninsula; in rain forests on New Zealand's west coast; in the open, lashed with sleet on subantarctic islands such as Macquarie and South Georgia; next to glaciers in the Antarctic, and, even, on ice. The one thing penguin nests have in common is that they are all at ground level. Although, even that is not always true: on the Snares Islands, the Snares Penguin nests within forests of olearia—small squat trees with chaotic branches. On the Snares, it is not uncommon for penguins to climb the branches of olearia trees and, occasionally, just occasionally, one might lay their eggs there.

The Antarctic has its advantages for penguins, but an equitable climate is not one of them.

The nest requirements for penguins, then, are quite variable and are influenced especially by latitude.

Q: How does latitude affect the breeding requirements of penguins?

A: Latitude affects penguins in a number of ways. First of all, at lower latitudes—those nearest the equator—it is warmer, seasons are less pronounced, and day length is less variable. As one moves farther south, it gets colder, seasons become more pronounced, the winters darker, the summers lighter. Until, by the time one gets to the Antarctic, it is not just cold, it is freezing; the window for breeding has been condensed into a few short months, but for compensation there is 24-hour daylight in which to work at being parents; all of which is followed by a period of complete darkness and bone marrow–freezing temperatures, when any animal in its right mind would get the heck out of there.

Except that one of them does not.

Q: Do Emperor Penguins really breed during the Antarctic winter?

A: If breeding in the Antarctic was not bad enough, Emperor Penguins go one step beyond the unenviable and into the realm of the incredible. In March and April each year, when other penguins, seals, and the flying birds have abandoned Antarctica to the icebergs, Emperor Penguins arrive at patches of frozen sea ice and begin a process of mating that will see them incubating eggs in complete darkness, at temperatures that can fall as low as −76°F (−60°C), but which can feel much colder, if that is possible to imagine, because strong winds plunge the wind-chill factor down to levels where the words *below freezing* take on new meaning.

Emperor Penguins nest on the sea ice, sometimes in the lee of ice cliffs that provide them a little protection from the prevailing winds. They do not bother with any sort of nest at all, but carry a single egg on their feet: eggs laid on the ground would freeze in Antarctic winter conditions. Freed of the normal spacing between nests that is characteristic of other penguins and colonial seabirds generally, the Emperor Penguins are able to huddle together, shifting positions within the huddle to stay warm.

By the time their chicks are ready to fledge, the sea ice is breaking up and other animals have arrived to begin breeding during the Antarctic summer.

Extreme breeders: Emperor Penguins do the incredible and breed during the worst of the Antarctic winter.

> **Take it all in all, I do not believe anybody on earth has a worse time than an Emperor penguin.**
> —Apsley Cherry-Garrard

Nesting in the Cold

Q: **What penguins breed during the Antarctic summer?**

A: Like the Emperor Penguin, Adelie and Chinstrap penguins breed exclusively in Antarctica, but they do so in the summer. In common with most other penguins, they lay their eggs on the ground. Their nests are shallow depressions that they line with stones. For them, the big problem is snow. The penguins tend to select sites for their colonies that are largely snow-free during the summer, often nesting on ridges. The stones allow any snow-melt to drain away, helping to keep the eggs dry.

Chinstrap Penguins, which breed during the long days of the Antarctic summer, line their nests with stones that allow drainage for any melting snow.

Stones therefore become a valuable commodity in such colonies, and are often in short supply. Even when they are not, rather than go and collect their own stones, Adelie Penguins and Chinstrap Penguins often steal the stones belonging to their neighbors.

Gentoo Penguins, which are closely related to the Adelies and Chinstraps, nest on the Antarctic Peninsula (that finger of Antarctica that points up at South America and was once joined to it) in part of their range. There they have nests lined with stones just like the other two species, but the Gentoo also nests in the subantarctic.

Q: **What are the nesting requirements for penguins in the subantarctic?**

A: Penguins in the subantarctic, as do those at higher latitudes, nest outside in the open. These latitudes are not called the Roaring Forties for nothing: the westerly winds are strong. To us, it may seem cold, but to the penguins sitting there in their feather survival suits, it is pretty much perfect. The downside of being dressed for krill is that being encased in something like a waterproof duvet when on land can become rather stifling without a bit of air-conditioning. The subantarctic winds provide that.

Gentoo Penguins that breed in the subantarctic line their nests with grasses or peat. Unlike the stony nests of penguins that breed in the Antarctic, which tend to be persistent from year to year, in the damper environment of the subantarctic, however, nests lined with vegetation can become fouled with guano and mud. As a consequence, Gentoo Penguins may shift the site for their colony ever so slightly from one year to the next in order to nest on areas with cleaner vegetation. Snares Penguins may do something similar. Others, such as the Erect-crested Penguin, are at the opposite extreme of penguin house-keeping in that they hardly bother with a nest at all: they are just as likely to lay their eggs directly onto rocks. The King Penguin has gone one step further, dispensing with a nest altogether and carries a single egg on its feet, just like its close cousin the Emperor Penguin. Given that there seems no rhyme or reason for the King Penguin not to have a nest, it seems likely that King and Emperor penguins have both derived this habit from ancestors that lived in extremely cold climates, much as the Emperor does now.

That is not to say that it is especially hot where King Penguins breed: other penguins nest in places that are much warmer than the subantarctic.

Left: King Penguins, like their close cousins the Emperors, have done away with a nest altogether, incubating their eggs on their feet.

Below: Gentoo Penguins breeding on the Antarctic Peninsula line their nests with stones, but those farther north use peat or grasses. Because vegetation-lined nests become fouled after a season's use, Gentoos move their sites slightly from year to year.

Nesting in Warm Places

Q: Why do penguins in temperate environments nest in burrows or under trees?

A: It was the advent of the feather survival suit, needed to keep a warm-blooded bird alive when immersed in water, that allowed penguins to cope with life in the freezer on land. They colonized the subantarctic. They emigrated to the Antarctic, with some even setting up camp there during the winter. Their feather survival suits made dealing with the cold easy. But the trouble with insulation that locks heat in when you are cold is that it continues to lock heat in when you are hot. For penguins breeding in lower latitudes, one of the biggest problems they face is insolation: heat from the sun. And if it were not bad enough that they were wearing a coat when the sun was shining, it is a black coat. To live in such climates, then, penguins must find ways of getting out of the sun.

The perfect nest sites for Yellow-eyed Penguins require plenty of vegetation overhead and around the sides. Their traditional habitat is forest, and above-ground houses of vegetation conforming to their specifications are sparsely distributed in the forest. The birds, therefore, tend to be sparsely distributed, too, often nesting tens and even hundreds of meters from their nearest neighbors.

Fiordland Penguins breeding on the southwest corner of New Zealand also nest in forest, in this case, rain forests, and they escape much of the sun's heat by taking a leaf out of the Emperor's book and breeding during the winter. Little Penguins escape the heat of the day in part by being nocturnal. They go ashore at dusk so most of their breeding behavior occurs with the lights off. They are quite flexible in where they nest, able to live in burrows and caves, or beneath bushes and rocks. Sometimes, in areas where their distribution overlaps with that of humans, such as at Phillip Island in Australia and Wellington in New Zealand, they can even nest under houses—much to the distress of the occupants. As romantic as it may sound to have a penguin living under your house, the reality sounds a lot worse; males serenade females during their nightly activities.

Fiordland Penguins nest in dense forest and begin breeding in the winter to escape the heat of the sun.

Q: Do penguins really breed in deserts and on the equator?

A: Although high temperatures on land present difficulties for a bird that is so well insulated, that has not stopped penguins from breeding in some of the world's hottest spots. If ever a reminder was needed that it is food that controls the distribution of penguins, one has only to consider the comfort of Humboldt Penguins breeding on the edges of the Atacama Desert in Chile. Nesting among cacti, they would surely die of heat exhaustion if they could not get out of the sun. They are there because the surrounding seas team with small fish such as anchovies and sardines, and, like all members of the banded penguins, they escape the sun when on land largely by living in burrows; although, where available, they will commandeer small caves. African Penguins also rely on burrows or, when they are not available, bushes. Studies on yet another banded penguin—Magellanic Penguins breeding in the windswept dry heat of Argentina's Punta Tombo (the site near to where Magellan and his men first encountered penguins)—have shown, however, that birds in burrows tend to do better than those under bushes. On the other flipper, burrows of African Penguins are more prone to flooding: reducing exposure to one menace can expose penguins to another. On

the Galápagos Islands, which have been formed relatively recently by volcanic activity (recent in geological terms means in the last five or six million years), it is often impossible for Galápagos Penguins to find suitable soils in which to burrow and they nests within cracks in the old lava fields. Simply getting out of the sun is not always enough, however, so penguins need to find other ways to regulate their temperatures.

Above: Magellanic Penguins and their ilk breed in hot South American environments by burrowing to gain protection from the glaring sun and high temperatures.

Left: Nesting in the sun in their beach habitat would be like wearing down coats on a tropical island—therefore African Penguins live mainly in burrows or under bushes.

Thermoregulation

Q: Why do penguins not overheat on land?

A: Contrary to our cartoon view of penguins bundled in knit hats and scarfs to survive in the cold, when ashore penguins mostly need ways to lose their heat rather than their cool. One way is to pant. If too hot, a penguin will pant, increasing evaporation from its mouth. Even penguins in the Antarctic may pant if the sun is out and the wind is absent.

Another option for hot penguins is to shunt their blood to the capillaries in the skin of their flippers and feet, which act like radiators. Heat-stressed penguins increase the efficiency of their flippers at radiating heat by holding them out from their bodies.

We regulate our body temperature by taking our clothes off and putting them on when necessary. Penguins cannot exactly do that with their feather survival suits, but they do the next best thing: they unzip them as far as they are able. Normally the feathers lock together, trapping a layer of air next to the skin. When the penguin is hot, muscles at the base of the feathers raise them, opening the feathers like louver windows and allowing the air to circulate. For penguins living in the hottest climates, however, even all of that is not enough.

Q: Why do some penguins have bare patches on their faces?

A: All four species of the banded penguins, those belonging to the genus *Spheniscus,* have bare patches of pink skin on their faces. These species, which live closer to the equator than other species, use the exposed patches of skin as heat vents. When the animal is hot, the face patches become infused with blood, which helps to cool the blood as it comes into near contact with the air.

The size of the facial patches varies between the species and is smallest in the Magellanic Penguin, which lives farther south, where it is colder, than do the other members of its genus.

Q: Is staying warm a problem for penguins on land?

A: Penguins can pretty much withstand the worst that the environment can throw at them. They can, of course, reverse any adjustments made to lose heat and, if need be, conserve it. If cold,

By extending its flippers and pumping blood through capillaries in its flippers and feet, the Macaroni Penguin can dissipate heat from its insulated body.

they shut down their peripheral circulation, they lock their feathers together, and they keep their flippers fastened to their sides. If they are able, they may even pull their feet up. When it becomes too windy, they will face into the wind if lying down and put their backs to it if standing. Adult Emperor Penguins huddle together for warmth during the Antarctic winter, but adults of other species are not into such close bonding and tend to maintain a personal space about them.

Their chicks, however, if cold and in a crèche with other chicks, will huddle in search of warmth.

Left: The banded penguins, which breed in the hottest climates, have bare patches of skin on their faces that are used to radiate excess heat.

Below: United they stand, divided they freeze: Emperor Penguins exchange personal space for warmth.

Coloniality

Q: Are penguins colonial seabirds?

A: Penguins certainly are colonial seabirds. Seabirds nest together because there are advantages in doing so. A colony makes finding a mate easier. It provides protection from predators. In some circumstances, it can help with finding food. Of course, if suitable nest sites are limited, congregations of seabirds could then be seen partly as a simple consequence of their all needing to breed in the same place. Penguins do not fit the classic seabird colony model well, however. Whereas colonial seabirds typically nest in one large colony, which minimizes the number of nests exposed to the outside, penguins most often nest in discrete subcolonies within a larger overall area that constitutes the colony. Subcolonies may come and go, expand and contract, demonstrating that the ground in between can be used for nesting.

Above: King Penguins in a colony on South Georgia number well into six figures.

Right: A juvenile male elephant seal is an unwelcome guest in a colony of Erect-crested Penguins.

Q: So why do penguins nest in subcolonies?

A: It is truly one of the mysteries that confronts a penguin biologist the first time he or she sees a penguin colony: If peripheral nests are more exposed, why do they not just all nest together, thereby minimizing the number of nests on the outside?

There is no really satisfactory answer. In part, it has to do with how much suitable terrain is available for breeding. Areas free of snow are more attractive to Adelie penguins than areas inclined to collect snow. Hence, they prefer ridges of land that tend to drain any snow-melt quickly should it snow; and ridges do not conform to the usual round shape of seabird colonies. Similarly, Snares Penguins require clearings within the olearia forest, and these are not unlimited in size. And Erect-crested Penguins nest on the limited faces and cliff tops out of the spray zone on the Antipodes Islands. But even given those limitations, there is space in most subcolonies to accommodate more nests: So why do the penguins persist in having more subcolonies and more exposed peripheral nests than they really need?

Another part of the answer would seem to be that large colonies are not obstacles to flying birds getting to their nests because they can hover and flop down on a nest no matter how far in from

Eggs and chicks on the outside of Adelie Penguin subcolonies are the most vulnerable to Skua predation.

the colony edge that it may be. On the other foot, a flightless bird like a penguin must walk from the outside edge into its nest, running a gauntlet of pecks and harassment from irate neighbors each time it returns home. There is some evidence that nests too far from the edge in large colonies of penguins may not be as good or as attractive as those just in from the edge. Nevertheless, in some species, individual penguin colonies can be huge. For example, on Deception Island, near the Antarctic Peninsula, colonies of Chinstraps may contain up to 150,000 birds and similarly sized congregations of King Penguins occur on Macquarie Island and South Georgia.

Q: Are Yellow-eyed Penguins and those that nest in burrows more solitary?

A: Penguin species that routinely nest in burrows—the banded penguins of the genus *Spheniscus* as well as Little

Penguins—do form aggregations of burrows as much as the terrain allows. Such colonies can number in the thousands. Yellow-eyed Penguins, although they nest in distinct areas that may be regarded as loose colonies, appear barely colonial in other respects: individual nests are so far apart that they cannot possibly offer any protection from predators.

Q: Do colonies really provide protection from predators?

A: Evidence from studies of Adelie Penguins has shown that eggs and chicks in nests on the outside of colonies are more than three times as likely to be lost to predators such as Skuas as those in central nests. The same even applies to peripheral nests in the burrow-nesting Magellanic Penguin. But for many penguins, predators are the least of their problems when it comes to breeding successfully: they have to find a mate first.

FINDING A MATE

For colonial seabirds, such as penguins, the difficulty with breeding is not so much finding a prospective mate—a major advantage of coloniality is that it brings together breeding-age representatives of each sex in the ornithological equivalent of a singles bar—but getting one of them to dance with you. In many birds, the males tend to be showy and compete among themselves for the attention of the females. In those species, males are not exactly homebodies and one male may have many partners. In contrast, colonial seabirds have to stick with one partner because both parents are necessary to raise young successfully. In monogamous situations such as this, pretty much all males get to breed and this reduces any advantages that being showy can bring: if having long tails or a fine coat gets you only the same number of girls as the guy in the scruffy shirt, then from an evolutionary point of view there is no advantage to getting dressed up. Consequently, monogamy leads to monomorphism, where males and females of a species look alike.

Undoubtedly, penguins do look alike: they are the icons for conformity, the unanimous ambassadors of the uniform. Until recently, then, it was assumed that penguins must go to the bar, fall in bird-love, and then mate for life. Wrong.

Above: Head pointed skyward, a Magellanic Penguin lets out a long call, proclaiming his availability to prospective mates.

Left: Male and female penguins, such as this pair of King Penguins, look alike.

Age and Aging

Q: At what age do penguins begin to breed?

A: As with many animals, body size has some effect on the time taken to reach reproductive maturity and to breed. The smallest species of penguins, Little Penguins, may breed first as two- to three-year-olds; for the largest, the wedding march of the Emperor Penguins usually occurs when they are five to six years old. But there is much more to it than that. Inshore-feeding penguins— the ones that tend to be resident at lower latitudes—breed at earlier ages than do equivalently sized offshore-feeding penguins, which are migratory and occupy the highest latitudes. The average age of first breeding for inshore-feeding penguins is three years, while offshore-feeding penguins wait twice as long and do not start the nuptials until they are around six. Of the latter, crested penguins take penguin virginity to the extreme: saving themselves for a remarkable seven to eight years.

Q: Why do crested penguins and other offshore-feeding penguins delay breeding?

A: Inshore-feeding penguins have less to learn: dinner is just out the back door. In penguin terms, it is a quick splash and dash to get supper or retrieve it for your offspring. For offshore-feeding penguins, the path to successful breeding is a bit trickier. You need to become an adequate forager, which means learning where to find the right food in the right amounts and how to retrieve it in the right way. And it is not simply a case of why not be in to win anyway; why not have a go as soon as you are able and learn by your mistakes? But investing in a failed breeding attempt impacts a bird's ability to breed again in the future; there are costs to failure. Evolution favors those who maximize their lifetime reproductive success: in such a scenario, refraining from breeding can be advantageous if, in the process, it makes you more likely to be successful when you do breed. But there is an upper constraint to that as well: longevity. There is no point refraining from breeding if the

Offshore feeders, such as the Magellanic Penguin, may not breed until they are six years old. In contrast, inshore-feeding penguins will usually begin breeding by age three.

environment you live in is so harsh that future opportunities to breed may be limited. Adelie Penguins, which must endure the miserable Antarctic winters, have—by penguin standards—relatively low survival rates from one year to the next and they tend to breed sooner than do the similarly sized, offshore-feeding, subantarctic crested penguins; perhaps because they die younger.

Q: How long do penguins live?

A: In June 2006, a banded Yellow-eyed Penguin was observed at Kaitorete Spit on New Zealand's Banks Peninsula. It had been banded as a chick, 171 miles (274 km) away on Otago Peninsula in 1982, making it at 24 years, 7 months, and 20 days, the oldest known-age penguin in the wild. Such records can only be obtained from long-term banding studies

and there are few to rival the yellow-eyed penguin study in length.

Body size is also a factor in longevity, with smaller animals tending to die younger than large ones. The longest a little penguin is known to have survived in the wild is 17 years, whereas from survival curves based upon an astonishing (given the conditions under which they breed) annual survival rate of 95 percent, it is estimated that a few Emperor Penguins probably get to celebrate their 50th birthdays. The oldest known Adelie Penguin made it to 20, but to keep things in perspective, we should remember that your average Adelie is lucky to survive its first year (only about half do) and, of those that show up in the colony as three-year-olds, half are dead by the time they are eight. In contrast to our own species, it is usually female penguins that die youngest, which affects the sex ratio of adults.

Little Penguins tend to die earlier than their larger cousins. Body size is a determining factor in how long a penguin lives, with smaller birds having the shortest average life span.

A long-term banding study of New Zealand's Yellow-eyed Penguins has tracked an individual penguin that has lived more than 24 years in the wild.

Sex Ratios

Q: Are there equal numbers of male and female penguins?

A: In 1930, a mathematician named Ronald Aylmer Fisher—perhaps wisely known to all and sundry as R. A. Fisher—proved that in sexually reproducing species where there is an equal genetic contribution from the father and mother (in other words, species like ourselves and penguins), natural selection will lead to a one-to-one sex ratio; put simply, equal numbers of males and

A group of African Penguins take a walk on the shore. Although natural selection favors a one-to-one ratio of males to females at hatching, by the time penguins reach breeding age, males will outnumber the females.

females will be produced. The proof is definitely not as easy to take as the pudding—unless you are one of those strange creatures that like a little calculus with your algebra—but essentially there will always be an advantage to producing the sex in shortest supply, so evolution tends to lead to systems that produce equal numbers of males and females. But it is one thing to have equal sex ratios at birth (or laying, in the case of birds), quite another as to whether the numbers remain the same as adults.

In penguins, females tend to start breeding at an earlier age than do males. Because breeding negatively impacts longevity—as any parent will tell you: kids take years off your life—this can lead to a male bias in the sex ratio of breeding adults. In Adelie Penguins, for example, an individual that starts breeding as a three- or four-year-old has little prospect of making it past ten, whereas those that delay breeding until they are six or seven, almost certainly will. Given that males are most likely to delay breeding, this means that within the colony at any one time there will be more males than there are females of breeding age. Additionally, because not all females arrive at the colony to breed simultaneously and males, on average, tend to get to the colony ahead of the females, this creates an even greater apparent sex-ratio bias at the time each female goes to breed. This is known as the operational sex ratio. For instance, say a female penguin arrives at a subcolony (distinct breeding group) at the start of the breeding season and there are ten males in the group but four are already paired. In effect, the other six will be competing for the amorous attentions of the female, so at the very moment she is about to make her choice, the effective sex ratio is actually six to one.

What all this does is that it creates competition among the males to get paired. In many monogamous birds there is an advantage to breeding early, with late breeders being less likely to have young that survive and go on to breed themselves. So, even though penguins are monogamous and most males will get to

breed anyway, there is intense competition to get paired as soon as possible. If there are characteristics of males that enable them to out-compete other males to get access to females or that make them sexier to females, then one might expect selection of those characteristics to lead to differences between males and females; what the scientists, with their propensity for big words, love to call sexual dimorphism.

Above: In a group of Snares Penguins, it is hard to tell the boys from the girls, but with over 25,000 breeding pairs on the island from which they take their name, there are males to spare.

Left: With males and females appearing so similar, just what traits will a female Gentoo look for among the males competing for her attention? It may be body size that determines her choice.

Sexual Dimorphism

Q: Are male and female penguins different from one another?

A: Although male and female penguins are extremely similar, they frequently differ in body size, with males being between 1 to 29 percent bigger in terms of body mass and size of features such as their bills and flippers. It is possible that selection for larger males arises because it gives them an advantage when competing against each other for assets such as the best nest sites that give them an "in" with the females, or (and these two possibilities are not mutually exclusive), because females mate preferentially with larger males.

Right: Although for humans thin may be in, a chubby, round fellow may hold the most appeal for a female penguin.

Below: A female Gentoo Penguin greets a male that has secured a nest site and lined it with stones. A larger male may be better able to protect a pair's nesting site.

Q: Is it likely females choose large males?

A: The phenomenon of female choice was, and still is, a controversial corner of biology. It is easier to show it occurs than it is to explain how or why it occurs.

This is especially so for species such as blue grouse in which the male's sole contribution to parenthood is to mate with the female, providing nothing more than his sperm to any female that will have him. In such circumstances, the females have been likened to shopping for genes: How, the theoretical biologists ask, can a female know that whatever makes a male attractive to her, will make their offspring more likely to survive and reproduce? Because, at the end of the day, that is all evolution cares about. If what you are doing, or what you have, does not improve reproductive outcomes relative to other behaviors or attributes, it will not prevail.

In species such as penguins, however, where the males must provide parental care, it is easy to see that if a female can select a male on the basis of some characteristic or marker that correlates with his ability as a dad, that should

convert into a greater number of offspring surviving and reproducing. Ultimately, that should lead to a proliferation of males with that characteristic, potentially making males different from females. If female penguins find big males attractive, that will lead to larger males, but that still does not explain why large body size should make a male a better father.

Q: Why should large body size of males make them better fathers?

A: Because all penguins have long incubation periods (it takes a month or more for the embryos to develop) and, when incubating, the bird on the nest cannot eat, it is too much for females to do alone in addition to making the eggs in the first place: males must help the females by taking their turn to look after the eggs. For inshore-feeding penguins, the incubating bird is left on the nest for only a day or two while its partner leaves to get food. For offshore-feeding penguins, the incubation spells range from one to two weeks, to over two months in the case of the Emperor. A key feature of any male's parental ability, then, will be how long he can go without food and remain looking after the eggs. Although human societies, especially in the West, have come to worship beauty in the form of the near-anorexic stick figures that we label supermodels, for a penguin, fat is beautiful. Bigger fat reserves mean that the bird can potentially remain on the nest longer, protecting the eggs and providing some leeway should the female,

when feeding at sea, take a bit longer to return than is normal. But how does a penguin assess condition? It is not like they can ask prospective mates to jump on a set of scales.

In Emperor Penguins, especially, fat is beautiful. It enables males to endure long periods of fasting.

Courtship

Q: How can female penguins pick large males?

A: In all penguin species, the males call in an endeavor to attract females. To use the singles bar analogy again, it is a bit like group karaoke. Males sing the same song and it is infectious: once one starts singing, his neighbors are often bound to join in. To our ears they all sound equally awful (imagine the gravelly voiced bar singer Tom Waits with a cold), but to penguins, in contrast to the uniformity of their dress (and visually, even penguins cannot tell each other apart), each one's voice is as individually distinct as a fingerprint. Bigger males tend to have deeper voices and, on average, are likely to have correspondingly bigger fuel reserves. There is some evidence that females prefer males with deeper voices, but if female penguins really want to choose the best males, it is the fat ones they should be after. A big skinny male will probably have fewer reserves than a small fat one. The voice box of penguins, known as the syrinx, is located in a region of the upper chest where it is overlaid by one of the penguin's primary areas for storing fat. It is possible that the more fat there is lying on top of the syrinx, the more it will attenuate—or flatten—the calls of a male. Although there has not been enough study to confirm or deny this, if what a girl really needs is a big fat male, female penguins should find a deep flat voice particularly sexy: imagine a courting Pavarotti with a cold.

A song only another penguin can love . . . an unattached male Gentoo calls to attract females.

Q: What is the courtship period, and how long does it last?

A: The courtship period covers the time from arrival at the colony at the start of the breeding season, through the process of pair formation and mating, to the completion of egg-laying.

Courtship typically lasts two to three weeks—although this can be variable depending upon how synchronous males and females are in their arrival at the colony at the start of the breeding season.

Q: How synchronous are males and females when they arrive at the colony for courtship?

A: In general, males arrive at the colony before females, although this is highly variable. In residential inshore-feeding species such as the African and Yellow-eyed penguins, where pairs may stay together year-round, it is academic as to whether one sex precedes the other. In the Antarctic-breeding Adelie, Chinstrap, and Emperor penguins, males tend to arrive at the colony first, but there is always over-lap, with some males getting there after the first of the females. In Magellanic Penguins and most of the crested species, such as Erect-crested Penguins, the males may arrive a week or more before the females. In these species, competition between males is strongest and it is notable that, in comparison to other species, males tend to have disproportionately larger and more robust bills relative to the females. Bills are used as weapons for fighting and it seems likely that the greater sexual dimorphism of bills in these penguins reflects the way evolution has rewarded males for possessing large bills, in the same way that it has favored large antlers in male deer. Such males get to the colony early

it seems to fight over access to nest sites, which, ultimately, gives them access to the females when they arrive.

Q: How do penguins know when to go to the colony to breed?

A: As with many birds, changing day length tells penguins when to initiate breeding. The pineal organ of penguins is sensitive to the amount of light and this in turn triggers hormonal changes within the penguins that tell them to return to the colony (if they are migratory) and to initiate breeding.

Above: A King Penguin pair bows to each other in greeting. Once they have arrived at the breeding colony, penguin courtship typically lasts two to three weeks.

Left: Once they have paired up, inshore-feeders, such as Humboldt Penguins, tend to stay together year-round.

The Breeding Season

A Magellanic pair in their burrow nest. One of the "warm weather" species, Magellanic Penguins breed from late September to February in the Falkland Islands, Argentina, and the bottom half of Chile.

Q: How long is the breeding season?

A: The length of the penguin breeding season is highly variable. There is generally a latitudinal relationship to breeding season length, with the period during which successful breeding can occur becoming progressively shorter the farther south one travels. The higher the latitude, the narrower becomes the window of opportunity for breeding, because the availability of food supply is more highly seasonal. This holds even within a species. For example, the laying of eggs of Adelie Penguins in the most southerly parts of their range occurs up to two weeks later than at more northerly Adelie colonies. At the other end of the scale, penguins breeding nearest the equator, although they do have peaks in breeding, can nevertheless breed year-round if conditions are favorable.

Q: Can penguins breed more than once per year?

A: Penguins in the lower latitudes, which have long breeding seasons (in other words, Galápagos, Humboldt, African, and Little penguins), may, if conditions allow, lay two clutches per year. What constitutes favorable conditions is probably determined by food supply rather than just latitude. Little Penguins breeding at the northern limits of their range in Western Australia (32°S) routinely lay two clutches, as do those breeding near the bottom of their range on New Zealand's Otago Peninsula (45°S), while in between, Little Penguins mainly lay a single clutch. Food, it seems, has a double impact upon breeding: there must be enough later in the season to feed chicks, but there must also be sufficient food for the birds to get fat enough to begin breeding.

Penguins typically lay one clutch of eggs per year, but lower-latitude denizens, such as the African Penguins, may lay a second clutch.

Q: Does the condition of a penguin affect whether it attempts to breed?

A: Although hormones are important to prime a penguin's reproductive system at the start of each breeding season, the birds must attain a minimum level of condition before they will breed. In situations where birds arrive at the breeding ground in poor condition—such as those years when persistent sea-ice means Adelie Penguins must walk much farther than normal across the ice to reach their colonies, using up valuable energy reserves as they do so—many birds will not breed. Similarly, in El Niño years in warmer climes, Humboldt Penguins and Yellow-eyed Penguins may skip a breeding season without attempting to breed.

As is nearly everything connected with penguins, breeding is a group activity and, somewhat surprisingly perhaps, encouragement from their peers helps ready penguins to breed.

Q: How does breeding in a group help prepare penguins to breed?

A: Penguins are, paradoxically, unsociably social. They congregate in colonies but act as individuals—even, selfish individuals. They steal nesting material and mates, and make no attempt to look after their neighbor's kids (in fact, they are just as likely to give them a flipper-bashing as a leg up) or their neighbor's wife (where a leg over is more likely to be offered than a hand). It is true that coloniality does offer benefits to penguins such as protection from predators and ease of finding mates, but one benefit less well understood is that social behavior helps stimulate and synchronize their breeding. Research carried out on the Royal subspecies of Macaroni Penguins has shown convincingly that the calling and mating behavior of neighbors helps to activate a penguin's reproductive system.

A group of Rockhopper Penguins. Although penguins are social birds that congregate in colonies, they act as distinct individuals, caring only for their own young.

Nest and Mate Fidelity

Q: **Where do penguins breed?**

A: Penguins are said to be philopatric, meaning that they generally go back to the colony in which they hatched to breed.

In a sea of calling penguins that all look alike, it is amazing that Adelie Penguins can find their former partners, but going back to their nest sites is a good starting point.

Once penguins have become established breeders, they normally remain extremely faithful to their nesting locations. Males are the most faithful to their nest sites, usually returning to the same one used the year before (that is, where they have well-defined and permanent nest sites). Yellow-eyed Penguins breed under vegetation and, although remaining faithful to a general area, the actual nest site may shift from one year to the next. The northern subspecies of Gentoo Penguins nest on peat and grassland that gets fouled by guano and so, as a consequence, the whole breeding group may move en masse by a few meters from one breeding season to another. Contrast that with the southern subspecies of Gentoo Penguins breeding on the Antarctic Peninsula: there they have nests that resemble the stone-lined depressions of the Adelie Penguins that, in places, they breed among. The southern Gentoos are not quite as site-attached as the Adelies, but they are a lot more so than their northern brethren. King and Emperor penguins have no nest and carry their eggs upon their feet. The King Penguins are territorial, however, so there is a degree of consistency from one breeding attempt to another in where they go; but Emperor Penguins do not even have a territory and move about. In penguins, because the nest site acts as a rendezvous point for ex-lovers, this affects the likelihood that pairs will reunite from one breeding attempt to the next.

Q: **Do penguins mate for life?**

A: Even when both members of a pair arrive back at the colony at the start of the breeding season, many do not reunite. In species such as the Galápagos and Yellow-eyed penguins, where pairs stay together year-round, up to 93 percent of pairs may reunite. In contrast, only about 15 percent of Emperor Penguins do so. It is ironic that the highest-grossing natural history documentary of all time, *March of the Penguins,* should have pitched the relationship between its main characters—Emperor Penguins—as a love story, when they have the highest divorce rate of all penguins:

85 percent from one year to the next! There is an excuse for the Emperors' fickle fidelity. The lack of a nest means that there is no rendezvous point for Emperor Penguins and they must rely on bumping into their old partners by listening for their calls. To get an idea of what it is like, imagine trying to find your partner at Yankee Stadium when nobody has seat numbers, everyone is dressed the same, and you are all calling out for each other at the same time.

On the other hand, if you had a definite seat to which you could return, then it would be much easier to meet up. Yet, even those penguins with permanent seats—or rather, nest sites—do not always reunite when both partners return. Up to 35 percent of Adelie Penguins, or more, may divorce in any given year. In this case, it is more about getting to the stadium on time than it is about finding a seat with your mate. Think of it this way: the farther south the penguins are breeding, the narrower is that window of opportunity in which to be able to breed successfully. The pressure is on to mate, with anyone if need be, rather than wait for a previous partner and risk missing out. Penguins breeding in the northernmost part of the Southern Hemisphere can afford to be a bit more flexible about when to start breeding and, consequently, divorce rates tend to be lower in the inshore-feeding residential penguins of the lower latitudes.

Yet, it is one thing to ditch a partner from season to season, but no one expected penguins to do it within a breeding season.

A Gentoo Penguin offers its mate a stone—a typical bonding ritual between pairs. Even though penguins are considered monogamous, divorce rates can be high for offshore feeders.

Changing Mates

Q: Can penguins have more than one partner in a season?

A: By observing the mating behavior of penguins continuously, penguin biologists have discovered that they lead remarkably varied sex lives. This was deduced originally from Adelie Penguins, where 24-hour daylight during their Antarctic summer breeding season was conducive to observing their breeding behavior around-the-clock for any biologist masochistic enough to do that, but it probably pertains to penguins generally. Rather than the romantic notion of a marriage for life, penguins are as prone to fluid relationships as are humans.

Above: Around-the-clock observation of the mating habits of Adelies first alerted biologists to the fact that penguins were not quite as faithful to their partners as had always been assumed.

Right: Thirty percent of female Humboldt Penguins cheat on their partners and engage in extra-pair copulations.

This can take the form of mate switching, whereby a male or female may have two, or even three, partners sequentially during the same courtship period. Most often this occurs when a penguin has paired with a new partner and the old partner from the previous season arrives. Females arriving at the colony to find their "old fella" already betrothed, will typically drive away the new female. Many fights that occur in penguin colonies during the courtship period are actually between females, though their sustained intensity makes them more catfights than bird fights; at least, not the gentle squabbles we might imagine bird fights to be. Conversely, a female that has hooked up with a new mate may abandon him for the old model if the previous season's male arrives afterwards (but not too late) and she has bred successfully with him before. In all this, the males are really passive pawns: they go with any female that will have them.

Another means of indulging in multiple partners is to have what is known scientifically as an "extra-pair copulation," although in humans we would simply call it an affair or, perhaps more accurately, a one-night stand. In this case the female does not transfer her affections from one male to another; rather, she has the briefest of flings with another male before returning to

in a penguin version of intimacy that is more shouting in the ear rather than whispering in it. Successful breeders get to have many nest relief ceremonies, but pairs that lose their eggs, for whatever reason, do not. This is especially so for offshore-feeding penguins; they are away so long at sea that they get to see their partners only two to three times during the entire incubation period. Absence may make the heart grow fonder in our case, but in penguins it just means that the head is more likely to forget. As a consequence, unsuccessful breeders have higher divorce rates, especially among offshore feeders.

Left: When an Adelie couple is successful at breeding one year, there is a greater likelihood that they reunite the next year.

Below: For offshore-feeding species such as King Penguins, the extended periods of absence from their partners mean that the pair-bond gets reinforced less often, contributing to higher divorce rates.

her original male. Because it occurs so quickly, this form of behavior went undetected in penguins for decades and has been documented only in the last little while. It may be much more common than we realize, however, with one study of Humboldt Penguins showing that 30 percent of females enjoy a bit on the side.

Q: Does breeding success influence whether penguins change mates?

A: Penguins are much more likely to change partners if they have been previously unsuccessful. Although it is tempting to credit female penguins with an eye for what makes the penguin equivalent of a good husband, whether they stay with a male probably comes down to something as simple as the number of nest reliefs a pair experienced in the previous breeding season. When relieving each other on the nest, partners go through an intense greeting ceremony, where they call to each other

Q: Are previously successful pairs likely to be successful again?

A: Although successful pairs are likely to reunite and it makes intuitive sense that what has worked once should have a higher than average chance of working again, the evidence is that penguins derive only a marginal benefit, if any, in terms of reproductive outcomes for their progeny.

Choosing a New Mate

Q: Why then do male and female penguins try to link up with a previously successful partner?

A: The advantages of reuniting with a previous partner may have less to do with enhanced prospects of breeding success than they do with avoiding the negative costs of finding a new mate. For male penguins, they could conceivably improve their reproductive potential by moving from peripheral nest sites to central ones (which are more successful in many penguin species), but they typically opt to stay where they are because the nest is the rendezvous point, the key to another liaison with their previous partner. Males that are divorced have a lower reproductive success than those that are retained, principally because a proportion of them end up missing out on getting a new mate. Females, while in stronger demand, can occasionally miss a breeding opportunity as well. This is particularly so when a female pairs with a male and his previous partner eventually shows up.

If a female cannot have her previous partner, she must choose a new one.

Q: What characteristics do females choose when getting a new partner?

A: When choosing a new partner, characteristics of males that you would think might make a male attractive—rather than just the way he combs his feathers—would be such things as whether he had been a previously successful breeder, whether he was known to the female, whether his nest was in a good location. Although age and inexperience do play a part, with females eschewing the new boys on the block for the older, more experienced types, the most crucial factor affecting a female's choice is proximity: she is likely to choose the nearest available male to her previous nest site. This has been shown in Adelie and Fiordland penguins, and likely as not it occurs in others. By doing this, a female is able to link up with a previous partner should he return.

For males, mating decisions are depressingly simple and stereotyped: a male goes back to his old nest site and

A Chinstrap collects a pebble. Male penguins typically return to their old nest sites, which they line with stones, and try to court females.

waits for the return of his female partner. In the meantime, he tries to shag anything that moves. For a female, she goes back to her old nest site and if her partner is there, she pairs with him; if not, she chooses a new male among those available closest to the old nest site. If the old male returns, she reverts to him as long as he shows up within a few days and they have been previously successful.

Q: Why might females choose to mate with more than one male?

A: It is easy, from an evolutionary point of view, to see the attraction for males that having an extra-pair copulation may bring: if they are lucky they will get to sire offspring that another bloke will rear for them, passing on their genes to the next generation for little effort. From the female's point of view the attractions are not so clear. She can produce only two eggs in a given season—whereas a male could potentially sire as many offspring as there are females that will copulate with him—and one male produces more than enough semen in a single copulation to fertilize them. It is possible that a female mates with other males as an insurance against infertility. It is possible that by mating with more than one male she increases the variability of her offspring, helping to ensure that at least some may have the right combination of genes to make them better suited to their environment. It is possible that by establishing relationships with other males, the female makes it easier to

The high rates of divorce in Emperor Penguins is a consequence of having no nest site and, hence, no fixed rendezvous point for pairs.

replace a male should her partner die or not turn up on time the next season. It is possible that the female is able to detect the best quality males and, by copulating with one of them, she can enhance the quality of their own kids while getting another male to rear them. But all this is pure speculation. The one thing that is clear: from the perspective of a male that is cuckolded, none of this is any good.

Why does a female penguin stray from her mate? There are several possibilities but little proof to support any of them.

Sperm Competition

Q: **What is sperm competition?**

A: When a female mates with more than one male and she has their sperm in her reproductive tract, there will be strong evolutionary pressure on the male that rears the offspring to do everything he can to ensure the resulting progeny are his. This type of competition that occurs between males after insemination is called sperm competition to distinguish it from the type of male-male competition that is a common part of sexual behavior leading up to mating, but really, from an evolutionary point of view, one is simply an extension of the other.

Males can compete against each other principally in two ways: by increasing the proportion of their own sperm in the female's reproductive tract or by ensuring that they are the last male to mate with the female, as it is often the last male's sperm that has precedence. Both mechanisms may play a part in the mating system of Adelie Penguins.

Q: **Why are Adelie penguins fitting species to study sperm competition?**

A: The mating behavior of Adelie Penguins is the most completely studied of any bird. This is because they are large birds that bred together in groups on the ground, in the open, under 24-hour daylight, which permits observers to see every mating of every bird throughout the entire courtship period. Not only that, it is actually possible to observe with the naked eye whether insemination has been successful (in other words, whether sperm has been successfully transferred to the female's reproductive system via the cloaca, the reproductive opening of penguins).

One consequence of becoming flightless is that penguins have lost the wings that flying birds often use to brace themselves when they mate. Couple that with an upright stance, short stubby legs, and a need to get down to the business end of the females after the male jumps on her back, and you have a recipe for chaotic and often incomplete sex. In about one-third of copulation attempts, males fall off the females. In another third, they miss their target. In only about a third of their attempts are males successful—which may explain, in part, why they try it so often.

The mating behavior of no other species of penguin has been more thoroughly studied than that of the Adelie. Because they breed during the 24-hour daylight of the Antarctic summer, biologists have been able to continuously observe them.

Q: How often do penguins mate?

A: In Erect-crested Penguins, males and females are lucky to get together every 30 hours or so. By contrast, in species where mate switching and extra-pair copulations are high, such as Adelie Penguins, the males copulate repeatedly with the females: about once every 3 hours for 12 days or so.

Q: So how do males counter the infidelities of their females?

A: If a female has mated with another male, the male that will rear the progeny does not increase his rate of copulations but does continue to copulate with the female for longer, thereby pumping as much of his own sperm into the female as he can. Eggs are fertilized about 24 hours before laying and although there is no peak in copulations around then, as might be expected in a bid for the sperm of the last male to have precedence, the last males do copulate right up until the second egg is fertilized (whereas in pairs that do not switch partners, sex stops the moment the first egg is laid).

Q: If males copulate so much, can they run out of sperm?

A: While we are often told that sperm are cheap—and relative to eggs, they certainly are—male Adelie Penguins sometimes do run out of sperm and therefore are infertile when mounting their partners. On the other hand, males engaging in a brief fling with another female that has sought him out for an extra-pair copulation, will preferentially allocate sperm to such matings.

But in case you think it is all fun and games: courtship in penguins is simply the precursor to months of toil that await them as parents.

An upright stance on stubby legs makes copulation awkward, if not downright clumsy. Males fall off females in one third of their mating attempts.

"It is not the strongest of the species that survives, nor the most intelligent that survives. It is the one that is the most adaptable to change."
—CHARLES DARWIN

CHAPTER 6

EGGS

Eggs are truly wonderful assets for flying birds. They enabled development to occur outside the parent's fuselage so that mom did not have to fly around with a belly full of babies. It is debatable, however, whether they are more help or hindrance to an aquatic bird such as a penguin because they tie it to the land. It is ironic that porous eggs enclosing warm-blooded embryos, which were one of the adaptations enabling flying birds to lift off from terra firma, should equally trap on land forever a bird that would be a fish. The eggs cannot be taken to sea; neither can they be buried on some beach like a turtle's eggs. They must be kept dry. They must be kept warm. In short, they must be incubated. But this creates a dilemma for the parents: the embryos take a long time to grow. It is too much to ask of one penguin to do all the parenting alone because, when on land, the parents must go on an enforced diet. The mom and dad, then, need to divide their time between the nest and the sea, but they must do this in a coordinated fashion; which is not the easiest thing for any relationship.

Above: After the female lays two eggs, the male Adelie then takes the first incubation stint, sitting on the eggs for two to three weeks.

Left: A Humboldt Penguin incubating its two eggs in the shade afforded by large rocks.

Clutch Size

Q: How many eggs do penguins lay?

A: With the exception of penguins belonging to the genus *Aptenodytes* (that is, the Emperor and King penguins), all penguins lay a clutch of two eggs. Young, first-time breeders may sometimes lay only a single egg. Emperor and King penguins lay a single egg whatever their age, which they carry on their feet. There have been isolated reports of naturally occurring three-egg clutches (as opposed to instances when two females may lay in the same nest), and there seems to be strong evidence that female penguins typically have three egg follicles (the precursors of the eggs) that start to develop but that the third one is not used under normal circumstances. Female penguins, however, can sometimes be induced to lay a third egg if the first one is lost or removed within 24 hours of laying.

Gentoo Penguins breeding on subantarctic islands use peat and grasses to make their nests, whereas those breeding on the Antarctic Peninsula use pebbles and stones.

Q: What is the laying interval between eggs?

A: The laying interval between eggs in a clutch results from differences in the timing of the development of the follicles. In essence, females cannot magically produce all the nutrients for all the eggs all at once: they make the eggs one at a time. Hence, in all birds there is a necessary interval between the laying of eggs in a clutch. In most penguins, the eggs are laid about three days apart, although this can be as high as four or, even, five days in crested penguins (where it takes longer to produce their larger second eggs).

Q: How big are penguin eggs?

A: The largest eggs belong, rightfully so, to the largest birds: Emperor Penguins lay eggs that are nearly a whopping five inches (12.4 cm) long, over three inches (8.4 cm) wide, and weigh more than a pound (469 g). In contrast, the eggs of Little Penguins are only two inches (5.5 cm) long, less than two inches (4.2 cm) in width, and you would need nearly nine of them to balance the scales with one Emperor egg.

Little Penguins lay two eggs, however, and, collectively, their clutches represent a much greater proportion of their body mass—about 10 percent of it—than the meager 2 percent or so that Emperor and King penguins invest in their single, albeit large, egg.

Q: Are eggs in a clutch the same size?

A: Given that a female penguin must essentially convert her body reserves to make eggs, it is perhaps not unreasonable to expect that as those reserves get used up, she might find it harder to stock succeeding eggs to the same degree as the first. In many penguins, the second egg tends to be either the same size or smaller than that of the first-laid egg. Of course, there are some fundamental requirements for eggs to provide for the nutrition of the developing embryo if they are ever to produce a viable chick and, for this reason, it seems that the amount of yolk in eggs is reasonably constant between first-, second-, and—where they occur—third-laid eggs. Differences that may occur in egg sizes within a clutch, then, primarily reflect differences in the amounts of albumin (that is the white stuff that surrounds the yellow bit when you are having your breakfast; except that

it only turns white when it is cooked). The yolk consists largely of fats, whereas the albumin consists largely of proteins. It is proteins that promote embryo growth, leading to larger chicks at hatching.

The eggs of such species as Chinstrap, Yellow-eyed, and some Gentoo penguins (depending upon location) show hardly any difference in size between first and second eggs within a clutch. Eggs of other gentoos and the likes of Adelie, African, and Magellanic penguins show a slight reduction in the size of the second egg, as if the female has trouble provisioning them to the same extent. The curious thing is that the eggs of crested penguins are quite the reverse: with the second egg being much larger than the first-laid egg.

Left: Although in most penguin species, there is little size difference between the two eggs of a clutch, with the second-laid egg the same size or only slightly smaller than the first, the situation is quite different for the eggs of crested penguins, such as this Rockhopper.

Below: The large second-laid egg and the much smaller first egg of the Erect-crested Penguin: the greatest difference in egg sizes found within the clutch of any bird species.

> **. . . a work of art, a masterpiece of design, construction, and brilliant packaging.**
> —Delia Smith, British chef, on the egg

Incubation Period

Q: Does the second egg of crested penguins develop faster?

A: Crested penguins not only fly in the face of trends in the other penguins by laying larger second eggs, but they also have the largest egg size differences of any bird. Erect-crested Penguins are the most extreme, with their second eggs being 85 percent heavier than their first eggs. This is primarily because of increased albumin in the second egg. In Erect-crested and Macaroni penguins, the parents do not even bother to look after the small first egg sufficiently, which is usually lost well before hatching; however, in the other crested penguins, even though the second egg is laid four days later, its chick develops faster and hatches first.

Right: A Humboldt Penguin egg, dirty after having been incubated on the ground for nearly 40 days.

Below: All crested penguins lay larger second eggs, and the size difference is most extreme in the aptly named Erect-crested Penguins.

Q: How long does it take to incubate penguin eggs before they hatch?

A: All penguins take more than a month to incubate their eggs and the length of the incubation period seems to be influenced as much by the type of penguin and its mode of incubation as it is by the size of the eggs. Little Penguins, the Pygoscelid penguins (Adelies, Chinstraps, and Gentoos), and crested penguins are the quickest, taking between 33 to 36 days. Somewhat surprisingly, the penguins breeding in the warmest climates, the banded or *Spheniscus* penguins, take longer to incubate similarly sized eggs (37 to 41 days), perhaps because the intensity of incubation in these burrow-dwelling penguins is less than that in penguins that breed in the open and must hunker down on the eggs to keep

them warm. Yellow-eyed Penguins are an anomaly all to themselves, taking an average of 44 days for their chicks to hatch; but this hides the fact that the incubation period in Yellow-eyed Penguins is extremely variable, ranging from 39 to 51 days. This is because they are not consistent with their incubation intensity and, sometimes, parents may even leave the eggs unattended for a day or two. King and Emperor penguins, which carry their large single eggs on their feet, take the longest for their eggs to develop fully: 54 and 64 days, respectively.

Whether they carry the eggs on their feet, or sit on them in the open or in a burrow, all penguins incubate their eggs by using an ingenious device known as the brood patch.

Q: What is the brood patch?

A: For an aquatic bird that uses its feathers as insulation to trap heat within its body, it has a potential problem when it comes to transferring that heat elsewhere. Simply to place an egg next to a penguin and expect it to be warmed would be like placing your hand around a thermos flask of coffee and expecting it to get warmed. If the flask is any good, then it simply will not happen because the insulation prevents the heat from being transferred from the coffee to your hand.

Penguins have got around this engineering difficulty by utilizing what is essentially a zippered opening to their warm skin, which in birds is known as the brood patch. At belly level and below, the feathers part to reveal a fluid-filled area of bare skin that becomes infused with blood vessels. Just as the sex hormones—testosterone and estrogen—control mating behavior, hormones also influence parenting behavior. Chief among these is prolactin and it is in response to increasing levels of prolactin that the brood patch develops. In some species that nest in cold climates and in the open, the brood patch develops quickly and leads to incubation from the moment of egg laying. In contrast, in species that inhabit warmer climes, the brood patch develops much more slowly over a period of days, so that initial incubation of the first-laid egg is incomplete. Laying asynchrony is a fact of life for birds, a product of the way eggs must be produced sequentially. By not incubating the first egg fully during that laying interval, however, this has the effect of delaying the initial development of the chick in the first egg so that the hatching of the chicks is more synchronous.

Recent work has shown that even just the sight of an egg can stimulate prolactin secretion and the formation of the brood patch: it is all part of Nature's way of switching penguins from sex-crazed machines to caring providers.

A King chick huddles beneath its parent's belly in search of warmth. While still in its egg, it had been kept warm tucked next to its mother's and father's brood patches—areas of bare skin infused with heat-providing blood vessels.

Incubation Patterns

Q: Why must both penguin parents rear their offspring?

A: Because the female penguin must devote large amounts of her energy and reserves to producing the eggs, it is impossible for her to sustain the fast needed

Snares Penguins nest in a shallow scrape on the ground that they line with twigs and small branches. Although the parents take turns incubating, for the first 10 days or so after laying, both stay together at the nest.

to incubate eggs in excess of one month. Consequently, although males contribute far less to the partnership up to the time of mating, evolution would not reward them for abandoning the females and seeking more inseminations (as it would if penguins were blue grouse), because none of their eggs would survive no matter how many inseminations they achieved. In other words, males have to help with the housework and the parenting, otherwise all miss out.

Q: How do males and females divide up parental care?

A: At the completion of laying, the female is usually the most exhausted part of the partnership, and will go to sea to find food, leaving the male to take the first incubation shift. Bizarrely, both male and female crested penguins, in keeping with their persona as the world's oddest penguins, stay together at the nest for a period of about 10 days, which is strange because only one bird can incubate the eggs at a time. You would think they should take the opportunity for one of them to go and get some dinner. In Chinstrap Penguins it varies as to whether the male or female goes to sea first. In Magellanic and all crested penguins except Fiordland, the male is the first to go to sea: This may be because the males in these species arrive at the colony well before the females, so by the completion of egg laying (or, in the case of the crested species, their joint incubation stint together), it is the males who are the most famished.

In the case of the six species of inshore-feeding penguins, males take the first shift incubating. But it lasts only one to two days before they are relieved by their females, who, in turn, have to sit on the eggs for only one to two days before getting another chance to feed. As a consequence, under normal circumstances incubating birds are not inclined to desert the eggs. If, for whatever reason, a partner does not return to the nest, the sitting bird will desert the eggs if left for six days or longer. Such desertions are, in fact, quite common in African and Little penguins.

Offshore-feeding penguins have to travel farther to get their food and, consequently, they are away longer, making the incubation shifts correspondingly longer, too. Excluding King and Emperor penguins, the first one of the pair to go to sea after laying is usually away for around two weeks (11 to 17 days), although Chinstraps take a tad under a week; when they swap over, the next shift is similarly around two weeks (10 to 17 days). King Penguins tend to be a bit longer than the rest: first the female is away for close to 19 days, with the males going subsequently for a similar period. Emperor Penguins are even more extreme. Emperor males incubate throughout the entire 64-day incubation

Inshore feeders, such as this African Penguin, alternate incubation shifts and feeding trips, which usually last a day or two, in concert with their partners.

period, leaving the females free to have a two-month sojourn to recuperate and stock up before heading back in time to feed the hatching chicks. Given that the males have already spent more than a month getting to the colony and during courtship, male Emperor Penguins must go without food, in the winter, in the world's harshest climate, for three and a half months.

While penguins can afford to divide up incubation duties any way that works for them, once the chicks hatch, everything changes because the chicks must be fed regularly and frequently.

Male and female Gentoo Penguins share incubation duties, making nest changes every one to three days.

Timing of the Incubation Period

Q: Can feeding penguins time their arrival back at the colony to be coincident with the hatching of their chicks?

A: There are some things in biology where it is easier to show something occurs than it is to know how it is happening. Female choice is one. Timing of the incubation period is another. It is possible to show statistically that feeding

Although it is not clear exactly how penguins know that their eggs are about to hatch, a study of Adelie Penguins revealed a rise in the level of the hormone progesterone in birds that were returning to the breeding colony in the few days before their eggs hatched.

penguins adjust their time at sea in relation to the time available until their eggs will hatch. It is not something peculiar to penguins either. Other seabirds with long incubation periods, such as the penguins' close cousins, the petrels and albatrosses, seem to do this too. But how? How does a bird miles from its nest know that its eggs are ready to pop?

Q: How do penguins know their eggs are about to hatch?

A: Like all biological clocks there is probably a hormonal basis to this behavior. All animals have circadian clocks: biorhythms that correspond to the 24-hour rhythmicity of the day-night cycle. Potentially any timer could work by counting the number of days that have passed since laying. But before we go crediting penguins with the numerical skills of Einstein, it is likely that any timer is much more simple than that. It probably operates like an oven timer: levels of some hormone change at a constant rate until reaching a certain threshold and triggering an alarm. We know that such a timer could theoretically be set by the dramatic drop in levels of the sex hormones (testosterone and estrogens) that occurs at laying. We do not know enough about the functioning of the hormonal system of birds, let alone penguins, to know what potential interactions of hormones could be involved.

In one study of Adelie Penguins, however, a rise in the hormone progesterone was detected in birds returning to the colony within a few days of their eggs hatching. Whether the rise in progesterone is part of an internal alarm system, a by-product of it, or an unrelated phenomenon is really hard to say at this stage. Whatever the triggers may be, penguins have evolved remarkably accurate systems for gauging their absences. Of course, they can sometimes get it wrong, with disastrous consequences.

Q: Why would penguin parents desert their nests?

A: An 11-pound (5 kg) male Adelie Penguin will fast for about four weeks from arrival at the colony for courtship until it is relieved by its partner after the first incubation spell. During that time it will lose about 30 percent of its body mass. It consumes energy at a steady rate during courtship and incubation, using up 1.7 ounces (50 g) of body mass per day, which is largely fat; however, when the penguin's fat reserves are exhausted to a certain threshold, which is about 20 percent of their starting levels, the penguin starts to break down its proteins to provide the necessary energy. Protein

is derived from muscle and you do not have to be an M.D. to realize that if you start consuming your muscles (literally eating yourself from the inside out), it will not be long before you deprive yourself of the very mobility that enables you to get food to survive. Hence, once they start burning appreciable amounts of proteins, hormonal warning bells go off in the penguins. Their own survival becomes more important than the fate of their eggs and they will desert the nest.

Initial studies of penguins did not observe them frequently enough to record how prevalent this was: researchers would simply encounter empty nests and would be unable to say what had happened, usually assuming that it was likely that predators had been responsible. It was only by closely monitoring nests that penguin biologists have discovered that desertions are a major cause of egg losses in many species of penguins, and especially in offshore-feeding ones.

Above: A male and female Magellanic Penguin sit outside the burrow in which they will take turns incubating their eggs.

Left: An Erect-crested Penguin sits on its egg. To ensure that it can go without food while incubating, a penguin must begin the breeding season with a healthy layer of fat.

Causes of Egg Mortality

Q: **How many penguin eggs are lost to desertion?**

A: In offshore-feeding penguins, as many as 15 to 20 percent of nests may be lost to desertions. The time a parent can spend on the nest, however,

The chances that a Little Penguin will desert its nest decrease when the food supply is close and absences from the nest by its foraging partner are shorter.

depends very much on the size of its fat reserves, which are in turn related to the food availability in a given year. Hence, the prevalence of desertions is highly variable from year to year. In years when food supply is poor or ice conditions prevent easy access to food, desertions may be higher. Poor food supply is a two-edged sword that affects both the sitting bird and the one at sea trying to find food. Incubating penguins in poor condition can sustain less fasting and will desert sooner; whereas anything

that increases the time taken to get food, such as poor food supply, will increase the time the feeding bird is away from the nest and the risk its partner will desert. Desertions account for 3 to 5 percent of eggs even in inshore feeders such as Yellow-eyed and African penguins. Little Penguins are somewhere in between: usually they adopt an inshore-feeding strategy and, in those situations, desertions affect fewer than 10 percent of eggs; however, in places where they follow more of an offshore feeding strategy, desertions may take its toll on as many as 28 percent of the eggs.

Q: **What are the other main causes of egg mortality?**

A: In some years, it is possible that desertions may be the major source of mortality, or at least one of the main ones. For a bird that nests upon the ground, however, predation was always likely to be a significant factor in its breeding success. This is especially so where there is predation by introduced mammals such as cats and mustelids (members of the weasel family). Penguins evolved their peculiar lifestyles in the absence of such predators and are poorly placed to deal with them now. In certain places, introduced mammalian predators threaten the long-term well-being of

whole populations, if not whole species. Of the natural predators, reptiles such as skinks can be an issue for penguins in isolated cases such as that of Little Penguins breeding in Western Australia: but, for the most part, the worst enemies of penguin eggs and chicks are other seabirds. Skuas, which look like large heavy gulls, can take up to 18 percent of Adelie Penguin eggs—although this varies from season to season and place to place.

Fighting, infertility, and flooding can all exact a toll on penguin eggs. And in some crested penguins (Macaroni and Erect-crested), parental neglect is a factor in the loss of the first-laid egg. Although there are many things that can kill them, one of the best ways of enhancing egg and chick survival is to have a central nest.

Q: How does nest location affect egg mortality?

A: Nests on the periphery of penguin colonies are most vulnerable to predation because they are more accessible to seabird predators such as Skuas, Sheathbills, Giant Petrels, and gulls. In one study of Adelie Penguin subcolonies (that is, the discrete breeding groups), more than 27 percent of eggs in peripheral nests were taken by Skuas, compared with less than 6 percent in central nests. And it does not seem to make much difference whether nests are aboveground or below: similarly, only 6 percent of eggs in central nests of the burrow-dwelling Magellanic Penguin were lost to predation compared to 23 percent in peripheral nests. And things do not get much better for the chicks when they hatch: chicks in nests on the outside of Adelie Penguin subcolonies were three times as likely to be taken by skuas as were those in inside nests.

Left: Fighting, infertility, flooding, and predation may threaten the survival of penguin eggs, but in Macaroni Penguins parental neglect typically accounts for the loss of the first-laid egg.

Below: A Skua makes off with an Adelie's egg. Nest location is crucial, with those nesting on the periphery of a breeding group being most vulnerable to predators.

Emperor Penguin

If penguins were people, then Emperor Penguins would be our royalty, Princess Diana in feathers. Beautiful, deliberate, and much admired, apart from their mode of reproduction.

SCIENTIFIC NAME:
Aptenodytes forsteri

Where is it found?
Found only in the Antarctic, this is the bird that defines tough, breeding during the Antarctic winter on frozen sea ice at about 30 locations around the continent. Emperor breeding sites are probably influenced by the availability of areas of open water, or polynias, during the winter.

What does it look like?
The Emperor Penguin is extreme in just about every way. It is, by a big margin, the biggest of penguins: 44 inches in length*, females can weigh up to 65 pounds while males can tip the scales at a creaking 84 pounds. If size were not enough to identify it, it has orange to yellow ear patches that fade into a broad swathe of pale yellow, which wraps down and around the upper chest. Otherwise it adopts the tried-and-true penguin attire of a black back and a white belly. Its bill is slender with an elegant curve, more stiletto than the broad meat-cleaver bills of some. Immature birds have a white chin in place of the black one sported by adults and their white ear patches only turn yellow as they age.

What does it eat?
Fish and squid are popular components of a well-balanced Emperor diet, with krill featuring quite often as well.

How does it nest?
The key to the Emperor Penguin being able to breed during the Antarctic winter is that it does not have a nest, opting to carry a large single egg, which weighs more than a pound, on its feet. This enables it to breed on sea ice and to huddle with others to stay warm in conditions that are beyond frightfully cold; they are simply frightening.

How many are there?
There are an estimated 218,000 pairs of Emperor Penguins doggedly going about the business of breeding in the Antarctic winter.

* **Birds are measured according to their length when lying down and stretched out, from their toes to the tips of their beaks. This is not the same as their height when standing, which is shorter.**

King Penguin

The Emperor may be the most regal, but the King Penguin that resembles it could claim to be the most glamorous. Its coloring is that little bit brighter, its demeanor that bit more brash.

SCIENTIFIC NAME:

Aptenodytes patagonica

Where is it found?

Restricted to a belt around the sub-antarctic, it can be found breeding on Falkland, South Georgia, Marion, Prince Edward, Crozet, Kerguelen, Macquarie, and Heard islands.

What does it look like?

Second only to the Emperor Penguin in size, the King Penguin is 37 inches in length and 32 to 35 pounds when at its best at the start of courtship. Its cheek patches are much more orange than those of Emperors, as is the coloring on the upper part of its chests. Its back is more gray than black. The plumage of juveniles is similar but duller than the adults, especially about the face, with the ear patches and upper chest being more yellow.

What does it eat?

The King Penguin is specialized to feed on fish of the open oceans—pelagic fish, as the scientists call them. Kings especially like lanternfish, which they dive to great depths to catch. They also take some squid. Penguins are visual hunters and it is likely that King Penguins rely on the bioluminescence of their prey to catch them as deep as 1,000 feet or more down in the murky depths.

How does it nest?

The King Penguin has a complicated and very unusual breeding cycle for birds, let alone penguins, taking 14 to 16 months to rear chicks. Consequently, King Penguins breed, at most, only twice every three years. They nest in dense colonies among tussock. Like the Emperors to which they are closely related, they do not make a nest but carry a single large egg on their feet. They do, however, have nesting territories, defending a patch within pecking distance of the others in the colony.

How many are there?

The worldwide population of King Penguins is estimated to be more than 1,600,000 pairs.

Adelie Penguin

T he explorer Durmont D'Urville named this penguin after his long-suffering wife, Adele, left behind in France.

SCIENTIFIC NAME:
Pygoscelis adeliae

Where is it found?
The Adelie is a purely Antarctic-based penguin. Adelies breed around the Antarctic continent and its associated islands, such as the South Shetland, South Orkney, South Sandwich, and Bouvetøya islands. They have the distinction of breeding farther south than any other penguin (indeed, any other bird), with the colony at Cape Royds (77°33′ S) marginally closer to the South Pole than the Emperor Penguin's most southerly location at Cape Crozier (77°20′ S), where, incidentally, there is also a large Adelie Penguin colony.

What does it look like?
This is the knee-high classic black-and-white penguin of cartoons. Adelies are 28 inches in length and weigh in at between 10 and 11 pounds when fighting fit at the start of the breeding season. Their most distinctive markings, apart from their black backs and

white fronts, are the white rings around their eyes. Feathers on the back of the head are somewhat longer than others and may be raised to form a small crest when the animal is aroused in some way. Juvenile birds lack the black throat plumage of their elders.

What does it eat?
The Adelie Penguin is dependent largely upon krill, and around the Antarctic Peninsula, krill can make up more than 98 percent of its diet. In other locations, fish and amphipods (small, shrimplike crustaceans) can also be important at certain times.

How does it nest?
The Adelie nests on areas of snow-free ground, lining its nests with stones. Colonies consist of distinct subcolonies or breeding groups, oftentimes on ridges or raised areas that readily drain snowmelt.

How many are there?
It is estimated that there are 2,500,000 pairs of Adelies dotted about the Antarctic.

Chinstrap Penguin

It is hard to see how any other common name would do given the striking plumage of the Chinstrap Penguin.

SCIENTIFIC NAME:

Pygoscelis antarctica

Where is it found?

Like its Adelie cousin, the Chinstrap Penguin is pretty much an Antarctic bird. Its distribution is concentrated around the Antarctic Peninsula and its associated arc of islands: South Georgia, South Orkney, South Shetland, and South Sandwich islands. Interestingly, small numbers breed on the Balleny Islands on the other side of Antarctica and on Bouvetøya, Peter the First, and Heard islands in between.

What does it look like?

With the exception of the Royal subspecies of the Macaroni Penguin, this is the only penguin to have a white face. But it is the strap of black that wraps around its chin, framing its eyes in a triangle of white, and all set off by the black bill, that makes it the standout of the Antarctic summer season. Thirty inches in length, and 11 pounds at its fattest, a Chinstrap is as svelte-looking as penguins get. Unusual for penguins, juveniles look almost identical to adults.

What does it eat?

The diet of a Chinstrap Penguin can be summed up in three simple words: krill, krill, krill. Forget a varied cuisine if you are a Chinstrap: 99 percent of what you eat will be krill.

How does it nest?

The Chinstrap Penguin nests on hillside slopes and rocky outcrops oftentimes in colonies that can be enormous.

How many are there?

The total population of Chinstraps is estimated to be 7,500,000 pairs.

Gentoo Penguin

This is in many ways an odd penguin: although its distribution overlaps that of its two close relatives, the Adelie and the Chinstrap, it extends much farther north and, in contrast to them, is an inshore feeder.

SCIENTIFIC NAME:
Pygoscelis papua

Where is it found?

Although found breeding around the Antarctic Peninsula, this bird is largely based in the subantarctic islands. In addition to the Antarctic Peninsula, the Gentoo Penguin breeds on Staten, Falkland, South Georgia, South Shetland, South Orkney, South Sandwich, Marion, Prince Edward, Crozet, Kerguelen, Heard, and Macquarie islands.

What does it look like?

Thirty inches in length and weighing 11 to 13 pounds, the Gentoo Penguin superficially resembles another inshore feeder, the Yellow-eyed Penguin, while being most closely related to the Adelie and Chinstrap penguins. Instead of a yellow stripe it has a white patch that extends behind the eyes and joins at the crown. Otherwise tuxedoed in the classic penguin manner, it is also distinguished by its largely orange bill.

What does it eat?

It is an inshore feeder and takes what is locally available. In the southern part of its range that means crustaceans and, in particular, krill. Farther north it relies mainly on fish, with bottom-dwelling fish that hug the inshore shelf its primary targets.

How does it nest?

In the Antarctic, the Gentoo Penguin nests on snow-free areas and beaches, using stones to line the nests like every other member of the genus *Pygoscelis*, but in the subantarctic it tends to nest amongst tussocks and uses peat and grasses to line its nests. Gentoo colonies can often be quite small compared with colonies of other penguin species.

How many are there?

There are currently somewhere in the vicinity of 317,000 pairs of Gentoo Penguins eking out a living around the southern regions of the world.

Macaroni Penguin

The world's most numerous penguin is actually one of the most puzzling, with nesting habits that border on the paradoxical, if not the pathological.

SCIENTIFIC NAME:

Eudyptes chrysolophus

Where is it found?

The distribution of the Macaroni Penguin is more skewed to the south than that of other crested penguins. It is found breeding from the subantarctic to the Antarctic Peninsula. In addition to the peninsula, colonies may be found on islands around Cape Horn, the Falklands, South Georgia, South Sandwich, South Orkney, South Shetland, Bouvetøya, Prince Edward, Marion, Crozet, Kerguelen, Heard, and Macquarie islands.

What does it look like?

As do all crested penguins, it has long feathers that look somewhat like eyebrows gone mad; in the Macaroni's case they droop down and, unlike the yellow crests of the other species, its crest feathers are orange. At 28 inches in length and about 11 pounds, it is the largest of the crested penguins. Those on Macquarie Island are distinguished by a white face and

constitute a subspecies known as the Royal Penguin. Some authorities accord the Royal full species status, but this seems unwarranted given that they freely interbreed with other Macaronis and behavioral, vocal, and DNA evidence does not suggest that they are distinct. Immature Macaroni Penguins are like adults but without the long feather crests.

What does it eat?

It is largely an eater of crustaceans such as krill, although, in some locations fish may constitute up to half of its diet.

How does it nest?

It breeds on rocky slopes and beaches. Some Macaroni Penguins make small nests of pebbles, mud, sand, or grasses, but many are content to lay their eggs directly onto bare rock. The first egg is tiny compared to the second egg and is typically lost before or on the same day the large second egg is laid. There

have even been reports that birds may deliberately eject the first egg from the nest, but it may be more a case of parental neglect than premeditated murder.

How many are there?

Although at around ten million pairs, they are the most numerous of the penguin species, there has been a substantial decline in their population over the last thirty years in some parts of their range, which is a cause for concern.

Erect-crested Penguin

These are the world's least-known penguins, the last to be the focus of serious study, principally because their two strongholds, the Bounty and Antipodes islands, are in the middle of nowhere.

SCIENTIFIC NAME:
Eudyptes sclateri

Where is it found?
It is largely restricted to the Bounty and Antipodes islands, which are hundreds of miles east and southeast of New Zealand, respectively. A few still remain in the Auckland Islands, but those that did likewise on Campbell Island seem to have packed up and left.

What does it look like?
Striking is the only way to describe the Erect-crested Penguin. Its most obvious feature is the set of upright yellow crests sitting above the eyes, like long eyebrows with an inordinate amount of hair gel holding them up. It is what other crested penguins would look like if they received an electric shock. Apart from that it conforms to the black-and-white penguin dress code. Juveniles do not have the long crest feathers and their throats are a mottled gray.

What does it eat?
Unstudied and unknown, it nevertheless seems certain based upon foraging trip patterns and comparison with its crested brethren that the Erect-crested Penguin must likewise eat mainly open-water crustaceans and fish.

How does it nest?
The Erect-crested Penguin breeds on rocky slopes close to the shore, laying its two eggs directly onto the bare rock in most instances.

The second egg is considerably larger than the first (the largest difference for any bird species) and the time between laying the first and second eggs, at five days, is also the longest laying interval of any penguin. Pairs only ever rear one chick, with the first-laid egg being lost within a week of the second being laid, and usually by the time the second egg is laid.

How many are there?
Although numbers of Erect-crested Penguins are tentatively put at about 165,000 pairs, this is likely to be a significant over-estimate because spot counts have shown worryingly high declines in recent years.

Rockhopper Penguin

These are the punk rock stars of the penguin world, where every day is a bad hair day. It is likely that Rockhopper Penguins consist of more than one species, with the Northern Rockhopper subspecies (or Moseley's Penguin, as it is sometimes called) deserving of separate species status from the Southern Rockhopper.

SCIENTIFIC NAME:
Eudyptes chrysocome

Where is it found?
The Northern Rockhopper breeds in cool temperate locations on Tristan da Cunha and Gough Island in the Atlantic and St. Paul and Amsterdam islands in the Indian Ocean. The Southern form has a circumpolar distribution around the upper part of the subantarctic, taking in the Cape Horn area, Falklands, Prince Edward, Marion, Crozet, Kerguelen, Macquarie, Campbell, Auckland, Heard, and Antipodes islands.

What does it look like?
The Rockhopper is a relatively small penguin at 24 inches in length and only six to seven pounds at its most puffed up. It has striking red eyes, but it is its chaotic crest that one immediately notices: at the back of what looks for all the world like a yellow eyebrow, long plumes of yellow feathers flail out in all directions. These plumes are longest in the Northern variety. Identification of juveniles is difficult.

What does it eat?
Crustaceans, especially krill, tickle the palate of a Rockhopper Penguin, though some fish and, to a lesser extent, squid may be used to round out the meal (although one study found squid was the major component of the Rockhopper diet).

How does it nest?
The Rockhopper Penguin really deserve its name, often hopping up rocky cliff faces several hundred feet high to nest on the cliff tops. Rockhoppers also nest on rocky slopes and among tussock. Nests are constructed of tussock, peat, and pebbles. Most of the smaller first eggs are lost sometime during incubation and, if they manage to produce chicks, the chicks usually die during the first few days of brooding.

How many are there?
Although there are about two million pairs of Rockhopper Penguins left in the world, they are classified as "vulnerable" because massive declines in their numbers have occurred throughout most of their range over the last few decades.

Fiordland Penguin

Although very closely related to the nearby Snares Penguins, Fiordland Penguins share something in common with Emperor Penguins: they breed during the winter.

SCIENTIFIC NAME:
Eudyptes pachyrhynchus

Where is it found?
The Fiordland Penguin is found breeding in the cold temperate rain forests on the southwest coast of New Zealand's South Island and Stewart Island, and the nearby coastal islands. Much of its distribution falls within Fiordland National Park.

What does it look like?
The telltale signs are largely in the crests, which look like thick yellow eyebrows that end with long drooping bits. It looks generally like a somewhat larger version of the Snares Penguin, although one thing that is peculiar to Fiordland Penguins is a series of white streaks on the cheeks that become apparent when the penguin is aroused. Otherwise it wears the black-and-white garb favored by so many penguins, fitted to a frame of 26 inches in length and a stocky 8 to 10 pounds in weight.

What does it eat?
The Fiordland Penguin has a variable diet. On the Fiordland coast, squid make up more than 80 percent of the diet, with crustaceans and a very small amount of fish serving as appetizers. On Codfish Island (near Stewart Island), however, small fish accounted for more than 80 percent of the food consumed.

How does it nest?
The Fiordland Penguin breeds in one of the wettest places imaginable, breeding under high rain-forest canopy beneath shrubs, boulders, or in caves. Colonies usually consist of loose groups, where nests can be several yards apart. Fiordland Penguins start breeding in June or July and, unlike other crested penguins, it is the female that takes the first trip to sea after laying is completed.

How many are there?
This is a notoriously hard beast to census, and counts have been few and far between, but it seems like there are something in the vicinity of only 2,500 to 3,000 pairs of Fiordland Penguins left. Unfortunately, numbers seem to be going down.

Snares Penguin

Their claim to fame is that they have the smallest breeding distribution of any penguin: they breed only on the tiny Snares Islands from which they take their name.

SCIENTIFIC NAME:
Eudyptes robustus

Where is it found?
The Snares Penguin breeds only on the Snares Islands south of New Zealand. In many ways the Snares Islands are a jewel in the subantarctic crown: pristine and heavily protected, they are free of the introduced mammals that have plagued other such islands. Landings on the islands are not allowed without a difficult-to-obtain permit and observance of very strict protocols.

What does it look like?
The Snares and Fiordland penguins are sibling species, meaning that they diverged in evolutionary time relatively recently. Visually, the Snares Penguin is like the little brother, which at about half an inch shorter, struggles to make 26 inches in length, and weighs somewhere in the region of 8 pounds. The Snares Penguin also has a white, fleshy margin at the base of its bill. Immature birds are probably almost indistinguishable from Fiordland Penguin youngsters.

What does it eat?
The diet of this penguin consists, it seems, of krill that is supplemented by squid and small fish.

How does it nest?
The Snares Penguin breeds in distinct, albeit small colonies in clearings amongst olearia forests and on open areas of rock. Although both chicks usually hatch, the small second-hatched chick (from the first-laid egg) typically does not survive for more than a few days.

How many are there?
With about 26,000 pairs of Snares Penguins, the species is not as bulletproof as those numbers may suggest. Their restricted distribution makes them especially vulnerable to any local catastrophe or environmental perturbations. The isolated and protected nature of their islands will not help in such circumstances and, really, there is a desperate need for more research on this species.

Yellow-eyed Penguin

SCIENTIFIC NAME:
Megadyptes antipodes

Where is it found?
The Yellow-eyed Penguin is found on the south-eastern coast of New Zealand's South Island, Stewart Island, and the Auckland and Campbell islands south of New Zealand.

What does it look like?
Given the literal naming practices of biologists, it would be surprising if the Yellow-eyed Penguin did not have yellow eyes and, indeed, it does. Stripes of yellow feathers pass from the eyes and join on the back of the head. It is a medium-sized penguin, albeit on the high side of medium at 30 inches in length and some 12 pounds in body mass. The young have pale yellow chins and their eye stripes are rather dull.

What does it eat?
The Yellow-eyed Penguin is an inshore-feeding fish-eater. It will take squid when it has to, but prefers bottom-dwelling fish or those found higher up in the water column.

How does it nest?
Traditionally the Yellow-eyed Penguin nests in dense forest. Where the forest has been destroyed, pairs frequently nest now on dunes replanted with native flaxes. Unlike other penguins, pairs typically nest many yards apart. Nests spaced tens or even hundreds of yards apart are normal for them. There has been some debate about whether pairs need to be visually isolated from each other, but it is likely that their distribution reflects the availability of suitable nest sites in the forests.

How many are there?
There are somewhere in the vicinity of 2,000 breeding pairs of Yellow-eyed Penguins, though accurate counts are unknown from their strongholds on the subantarctic Campbell and Auckland islands. On the New Zealand mainland and Stewart Island, census results have tended to waver between the not-so-good news and the bad news.

Often touted as the world's rarest penguin—a claim they no longer deserve, which unfortunately has less to do with a resurgence in their numbers than it has with a tragic decline in the population of Galápagos Penguins—they can still claim to be the world's least-social penguin.

Little Penguin

This penguin goes by a variety of aliases—Blue Penguin, Fairy Penguin, and Little Blue Penguin—though given its small stature, Little Penguin really does seem the most appropriate.

SCIENTIFIC NAME:
Eudyptula minor

Where is it found?
The Little Penguin is widely distributed around the bottom half of Australia and virtually the whole of New Zealand. There are six subspecies recognized, and for a long while some argued for separate species status for the White-flippered Penguin, a variety of the Little Penguin that has—predictably—white flippers (more like a stripe of white on the back of the flippers). DNA evidence, however, has shown that they are freely interbreeding members of Little Penguin society.

What does it look like?
This is a tiny penguin, probably as tiny as penguins have ever been, being not much more than two pounds in weight and struggling to make 16 inches in length. It has a white belly *à la* the penguin code of dress, but instead of black, its back is blue, which can vary from a pale blue through to a dark slate blue.

What does it eat?
The Little Penguin likes little fish, especially sardines and anchovies, although it will also take some squid and crustaceans when pressed.

How does it nest?
Unlike other penguins, the Little Penguin is largely a nocturnal creature when it comes to its onshore habits, waiting until after dusk to come ashore and generally leaving to go and feed before dawn. Pairs nest in burrows, in crevices, in caves, and under trees. Nests are usually clustered near each other.

How many are there?
For such a little bird living in association with humans, there are a lot of them, an estimated 250,000 pairs—perhaps night-shift work and living underground has its benefits after all.

African Penguin

Probably the first penguin encountered by Europeans, it is also the only penguin found near the African continent, where it has gone by the names Jackass Penguin and Black-footed Penguin at various times.

SCIENTIFIC NAME:
Spheniscus demersus

Where is it found?

Native to southern Africa, African Penguin colonies are found particularly where the Benguela Current brings cold, nutrient-rich waters to the southern and west coast of South Africa and Namibia.

What does it look like?

As one of the so-called "banded penguins," those members of the genus *Spheniscus*, the African Penguin can be distinguished from the somewhat similar Magellanic Penguin by its single black breast band compared to the latter's two. Otherwise, it has a black face and a patch of bare skin around the eye, a black back, and a white belly that may have a variable number of black spots. All this is packaged within a 27-inch frame in length, weighing six or seven pounds. Immature birds look not unlike Little Penguins and have a gray face.

What does it eat?

It feeds mainly on fish, especially anchovy, but will also eat squid and crustaceans.

How does it nest?

The African Penguin nests in burrows and otherwise gets out of the fierce African heat under shrubs or in rock crevices. Depending upon conditions, it is potentially able to breed at almost any time of the year, making breeding less synchronized than it is for other penguins. There do, however, tend to be breeding peaks at mid-year and near the end of the year.

How many are there?

Following massive declines over the last century, there are now said to be only about 56,000 pairs of African Penguins left.

Magellanic Penguin

Closely related to the African Penguin, Magellanic Penguins breed all the way on the other side of the Atlantic, where they are distinguished by being the only migratory offshore-feeding members of the banded penguins.

SCIENTIFIC NAME:

Spheniscus magellanicus

Where is it found?

The Magellanic Penguin breeds around the southern tip of South America, from 40°S on the Argentine side of the continent to 37°S on the Chilean side, and including the Falkland Islands. It is on the Argentine side where it is most populous.

What does it look like?

Twenty-eight inches in length and 10 or 11 pounds, the Magellanic Penguin is a middle-weight penguin, distinguishable from other banded penguins by the double chest bands (a thick black band around the throat and a thinner one farther down on the chest proper). The patch of bare skin around the eye also tends to be much reduced, consistent with it being the most southerly living of the banded penguins and, therefore, exposed to cooler climates. As with all juveniles of banded penguins, they tend to resemble gray forms of the Little Penguin.

What does it eat?

The Magellanic Penguin is largely a fish-eater and has a hook at the end of its bill to prove it, which is used to grasp the fish that it catches. When handling penguins, one needs to be wary of such weapons. The Magellanic Penguin, as are most penguins, is an opportunistic feeder and will take squid and crustaceans at times.

How does it nest?

The Magellanic Penguin breeds in burrows where digging is possible, otherwise it nests under bushes. Unusually, males arrive at the colony in September to October, more than two weeks before the females.

How many are there?

With a population of 1.3 million pairs, these are by far and away the most numerous of the banded penguins.

Humboldt Penguin

These are penguins that give the lie to the popular misconception that penguins are creatures of the snow and ice: Humboldt Penguins may be found living in the coastal suburbs of real deserts, sharing their terrain with cacti.

SCIENTIFIC NAME:
Spheniscus humboldti

Where is it found?
It is found on the western side of South America in the path of the cold, nutrient-bearing Humboldt Current, nesting from 42°S in Chile to as far north as 5°S in Peru.

What does it look like?
The Humboldt Penguin is distinguishable from the Magellanic Penguin, which it overlaps in range to a limited extent, in that it has only a single black band across the chest. It also has a much more extensive area of bare pink skin around the base of the bill than do Magellanic Penguins or, indeed, any of the other banded penguins. Otherwise it is a similar size, stepping up to the scales at 10 or 11 pounds, which is carried on its 28-inch-length body.

What does it eat?
Small schooling fish, such as sardines and anchovies, are its staple diet, supplemented with the odd squid. The availability of its food is particularly affected by El Niño events.

How does it nest?
The Humboldt Penguin nests in burrows (which in some places may be dug into guano deposits), among boulders, or in sea caves—anywhere it can get a little shade. Potentially pairs are able to breed throughout the year, although there are two definite peaks and, unlike most other penguins, many Humboldt Penguins produce two clutches per year.

How many are there?
These are birds that have been seriously persecuted over the years, by both humans and the vagaries of their environment. Estimates put the world population at about 13,000 birds, however, a recent reassessment of numbers of Humboldt Penguins on Isla Chañaral, Chile, found that there were 22,000 there alone. So although the Humboldt remains in jeopardy, it would seem that the situation is not quite as dire as had been imagined.

Galápagos Penguin

These penguins are real enigmas compared with their cartoon persona: they are not found at the South Pole but instead breed on the equator.

SCIENTIFIC NAME

Spheniscus mendiculus

Where is it found?

Restricted to the Galápagos Islands, some 600 miles from Ecuador, the Galápagos Penguin breeds on the islands of Isabela, Fernandina, and possibly Bartholome.

What does it look like?

The Galápagos Penguin is a quite small penguin at only 19 inches in length and 4 or 5 pounds in weight. Proportionally, however, it has a relatively large bill and the white line that surrounds its black face is thinner than that on other banded penguins.

What does it eat?

The Galápagos Penguin generally eats only fish for its appetizer, main course, and dessert. Sardines and mullet are favorites.

How does it nest?

The Galápagos Penguin manages to turn the remnants of the seriously hot into cooling shade so that it can breed on the equator:

it nests within crevices and caves in the lava from old volcanic eruptions. Elsewhere, where it can, it burrows.

How many are there?

This is the world's most precarious population of penguins. There are probably less than 1,500 pairs today and tomorrow there are likely to be fewer still. In a place celebrated for its giant tortoises and drab finches—because of their importance to Charles Darwin's theory of natural selection—the Galápagos Penguins sadly do not get the attention they deserve.

CHAPTER 7

CHICKS

When penguin chicks hatch, they are described by scientists as "semiprecocial," which is a polite way of saying that they are half helpless. They are essentially all feet and stomach. The feet make them mobile enough to move about the nest, but that is about as far as they go when it comes to fending for themselves. Their stomachs are the part of their anatomy that demands the most attention and it becomes the parents' job to keep them quiet by getting food and stuffing those stomachs full. For the first two to three weeks

of their lives, chicks are dependent upon their parents to not only feed them but also to keep them warm and to protect them from predators. This requires one parent to stay with the chicks at all times. But, at a certain point, the demands of the growing chicks make it necessary for both parents to be away from the nest simultaneously to collect food.

In effect, parents and chicks are taking part in a race: against time, against the prospect of a dwindling seasonal food supply, against a change in the weather. At the end of the day, or perhaps that should be season, the only good chick is a fat chick; the skinny will not survive.

Above: Safety in numbers: during the absences of their foraging parents, Emperor Penguin chicks congregate in crèches.

Left: A King Penguin chick sports a thick, downy coat, looking for all the world like a "mutant teddy bear."

Hatching

Little more than a stomach on feet, newly hatched Adelie chicks are covered in gray down.

Q: **How do chicks hatch?**

A: Baby penguin chicks have what is known as an egg tooth, which is a hardened white toothlike tip on the upper part of their bill. When they are ready, they use this to batter a hole in the side of the egg. Once the initial hole in the egg is made, it may take a day for the chick to extricate itself completely from the egg. For the day or so before it hatches, the chick may be heard cheeping. At this time the parent will often lean down and give what are known as loud mutual calls to the eggs. These are similar "bonding" calls to those that serve to reinforce the pair-bond between mates.

they hatch, but this fades to an all-over uniform slate gray in older chicks. Gentoo chicks have fluffy gray backs with paler fronts. Parents will brood the chicks for the first 15 days or so, which is the time it takes for the chicks to develop to a stage where they are able to fully regulate their own body temperatures.

An Adelie chick just beginning to work its way out of its egg. Using its "egg tooth," a toothlike tip on the upper part of its bill, it can take at least a day for it to batter its way out of the shell.

Q: **Are chicks naked when they hatch?**

A: Penguin chicks hatch covered in a thick layer of down. Although more independent than, say, a sparrow's chicks, they are not by any means independent and would die in a heart-beat if it were not for the attentions of their parents. Chicks of Adelie Penguins have a black cap of down when

Q: **What is the hatching interval?**

A: Although eggs of penguins are laid three to five days apart, the hatching interval is usually much reduced because of incomplete incubation of the first egg until laying is completed. In penguins such as the Adelie, the first chick hatches only a day or so in advance of its sib. In Yellow-eyed Penguins, both chicks usually hatch on the same day, and in crested penguins, the situation is reversed: the chick from the larger second-laid egg develops faster and hatches before the chick from the first-laid egg. This seems to be due to a combination of factors: the large egg has more albumin and, hence, more proteins important for development; there is delayed brood patch development and the first egg is pretty much neglected until the second is laid; and, it seems that the larger egg gets the preferential posterior position when being incubated against the brood patch.

Q: What is the yolk sac?

A: The yolk sac is the part of the egg that contains the yolk used to sustain the developing embryo. By the time the chick is ready to hatch, the yolk sac is internalized as a temporary extension of the gut; however, not  all the yolk is used up by the time of hatching and there remains enough so that the chicks can survive for up to six days without being fed. The yolk sac, then, provides the chicks with a measure of insurance if a parent is tardy getting back to the nest with food when the chick hatches.

Q: What is esophageal milk?

A: This is a secretion that is produced by incubating male Emperor Penguins to feed their newly hatched chicks if the mother has yet to arrive back from her time at sea: Even though the fathers have gone without food themselves for over three months, they can make the milk by breaking down tissues in their throats. Emperors have, in effect, double insurance: the yolk sac in the chick and the milk in the dad. King Penguins also have double insurance, but instead of the males making milk they are able to suppress their digestive system and store food in their stomach for several weeks as a hedge against the late return of their female partner at the time their chick hatches. Even so, Emperor and King chicks, just like other penguins chicks, are not immune to starvation.

Left: An egg's yolk sac becomes a temporary extension of the chick's gut, and may provide it sustenance for up to six days after hatching.

Below: A Gentoo Penguin guarding its chicks. The chicks are guarded on their stony nest for up to 30 days before venturing out to join crèches while both parents get food.

Chick Mortality

Q: How many chicks die of starvation?

A: During incubation, the danger for a feeding penguin that takes too long at sea is that its partner might exhaust its fat reserves and desert the nest. Closer to hatching, however, that danger is much diminished because by then both members of the pair will have had an opportunity to go to sea and replenish their reserves. The risk for a late bird is not that its partner will desert but that its chicks will hatch and, without food soon after hatching, they will starve to death. Although penguins seem to have an inbuilt timer that lets them know when to get back to the nest about the time their chicks will hatch, the risks of starvation then are high, especially for offshore feeders. The peak in starvations for Adelie penguin chicks occurs when they are six days old: the contents of their yolk sac have been exhausted and the parent at sea has not returned to feed them. Up to one in eight Adelie chicks die of starvation, most often because they have never received their first feed.

In contrast, for inshore-feeding penguins, which take only short absences from the nest, the likelihood is that a parent will be there to feed hatching chicks within the window that the yolk sac provides. As a consequence, starvations are not really an issue for the newly hatched chicks. On the other hand, while one of the advantages for inshore-feeding penguins is that they have a nearby source of food that tends to be available year-round, the disadvantage is that productivity is generally flatter compared to the enormous seasonal peaks in productivity at high latitudes that are the domain of the offshore feeder. As the chicks of inshore feeders grow bigger and develop more demanding needs, it can, depending upon conditions, become difficult for parents to get enough fish to feed their chicks. The chicks of inshore-feeding penguins, as a result, are most at risk from starvation after six to eight weeks of age.

Starvation is a primary cause of death for chicks of Snares, Fiordland, and Rockhopper penguins, but in these crested penguins it is neither a matter of the timing of the parent's return, nor the available food supply at sea: death occurs when the chicks are young and their food demands are relatively modest. The

A bedraggled Gentoo chick awaits a meal. The risk of starvation always looms before penguin chicks.

Shedding its down, a King Penguin chick, at right, stands as tall as its parent. It has managed to successfully navigate the many hazards of early life.

18 days. Diseases can potentially be a factor in penguin deaths and have been implicated in cases of mass deaths of penguin chicks that have occurred in Antarctica with Adelie Penguin chicks and in New Zealand with Yellow-eyed Penguin chicks. Relatively little is known, however, of the prevalence of disease in penguins. But without a doubt, the major threat faced by chicks is predation.

culprits are their older brothers or sisters: the first-hatched chick (which in crested penguins comes from the second-laid egg) out-competes the smaller second-hatched chick, monopolizing the food brought by their moms. It is yet another bizarre feature of crested penguins that during the period when the chicks must be guarded, the father does all the guarding while the mother does all the gathering of the food and preparing of the meals: the feminist movement has apparently not penetrated the world of the crested penguins.

Q: What are the other threats to penguin chicks?

A: For burrow-nesting penguins, burrow collapse and flooding can be significant causes of chick loss. Getting wet and cold can kill African Penguin chicks, especially during the first 10 days of their lives and, for the smaller Little Penguins, the chicks are vulnerable up to

Regular feeds can reduce the risk of starvation for Adelie chicks, but there are other threats to their well-being, too.

Predation and Protection

Q: **What penguin chicks are most vulnerable to predation?**

A: As with eggs, the natural predators of the penguins are other birds such as Skuas and Giant Petrels. These are seabirds adapted for catching fish, not dispatching penguin chicks. Introduced stoats and ferrets, which have devastated New Zealand's birdlife (including its penguins), have been labeled "innocent killers." In that case, Skuas deserve to be called "inefficient killers." It can take up to half an hour for a pair of Skuas working in tandem to kill a large Adelie Penguin chick. And yet, some Skuas breeding within penguin colonies have come to rely on penguin chicks for sustenance. In one study, up to 23 percent of Adelie chicks were killed by Skuas. Southern Giant

Petrels may kill more than 11 percent of King Penguin chicks, and they will even take isolated Emperor Penguin chicks.

Chicks are vulnerable until they are big enough to fend off the predators by themselves. The risk of predation is most apparent when the chicks are small and being guarded (and, just like the eggs, it is the chicks on the periphery of breeding groups that are most at risk), as well as during the initial period when they are left unguarded.

Q: **What is the guard stage?**

A: The semihelpless state of penguin chicks means that they must be brooded for the first two or three weeks of their lives by having one parent on the nest with the chick at all times (in Emperor and King penguins, the chick is carried on the feet). The presence of the parent provides warmth for the chick, which cannot fully thermoregulate its own body temperature, protects it from predators and, of course, feeds it when it demands food. This period is known as the guard stage and, in most penguins, parents have a ceremonious changing of the guard at the nest every day or so. Crested penguins, of course, do it their own way, with the males guarding the chicks throughout the guard stage. Emperor

Working together, one Skua distracts the incubating Rockhopper Penguin while its partner moves in to pounce on the egg.

Penguins are also different: the male does all the incubation and, when the female arrives and relieves him, she broods and feeds the chick for 24 days while the male goes to sea to feed. She can do this because she stores food in her stomach and is able to refrain from digesting it.

Above: A Giant Petrel in flight. Emperor Penguins, which live in the most inhospitable environment imaginable, have few terrestrial predators, but Giant Petrels take a toll on their chicks.

Left: Adapted to catching fish, Skuas are inefficient killers. Two Skuas can take up to a half hour to kill an Adelie chick, such as this one that was nearly ready to fledge.

Below left: At about three weeks of age, fast-growing Adelie chicks need more food than one parent can supply, so mom and dad must leave them unguarded.

Q: **Why do penguins parents leave their chicks unguarded?**

A: In short, as chicks get bigger, they need more food. At a certain point it becomes more efficient for both parents to be hunting for food at the same time, but this means leaving the chicks alone.

The period after which chicks are left by themselves is known, with all the romance for which penguin biologists are famous, as the postguard stage, but if the chicks have access to others they will often form crèches, so it is not uncommon to hear it referred to as the crèching stage, too.

Crèching and the Postguard Stage

Q: What is a crèche?

A: A crèche is a congregation of chicks. Typically they occur within the confines of the breeding group and, technically, when there are three or more chicks in close proximity that could be called a crèche. Usually, however, there will be several to many chicks standing or lying around together like a pack of unemployed youths, which is essentially what they are. Their job is to wait for their next meal and to try to stay safe. Originally it was thought that chicks congregate for warmth, but although they will clump together if weather conditions turn unfavorable, for the most part they hang together without contact. Crèches function mainly for protection and the prevalence of crèching is linked to the number of adults present in the colony. If there are plenty of adults, the chicks do not crèche and instead mingle with the adults, who by their very presence provide passive protection from the likes of Skuas.

In Adelie Penguins, coincident with the chicks first being left unguarded there is an influx of adult penguins to the colony in a phenomenon labeled, again with a deft touch, the reoccupation period.

Q: What is the reoccupation period?

A: Adelie Penguins that fail to find a mate during courtship, or fail to look after their eggs adequately, disappear off to sea to fatten up but, like magic, return to the colony just as the successful parents are going into overdrive and abandoning their chicks to their own devices as they go off to forage diligently for their chicks' suppers. These loser penguins then set about going through all the rituals that breeding normally entails: establishing nest sites, courting females, forming liaisons, and

African Penguin chicks. The period, when both parents must be away from the nest simultaneously to find sufficient food, is known as the postguard stage.

A crèche of Adelies. Penguin chicks have little to do but stay safe until their next feeding, therefore, the fewer the adults present in a colony, the more inclined the chicks are to crèche.

even copulating. All for naught. There are no progeny and there is no evidence that the liaisons formed during the playacting of the reoccupation period are likely to be rekindled during the next real breeding season. It is as if planned parenthood requires practice and the practice itself is reward enough for these birds.

A consequence of these adults being present in the colony is that they provide passive protection for the chicks from predators. It is not as if they act as a police force or body guards, but just their mere presence intimidates potential predators such as Skuas, and the adult penguins will often chase Skuas that come too close to them. From the point of view of chicks, it does not matter why the adult is chasing the Skua because the end result is the same: a chick that stands near to an adult has a better chance of not enduring a slow and painful death.

This reoccupation period lasts about two weeks and, by the time all the failed breeders have gone, the chicks are pretty much able to stand up to Skuas on their own as they resolutely pursue their job: waiting for their parents to feed them.

A Skua glides on past King Penguin chicks, which are too big to be bothered by it, as they stand with two adults.

Feeding

Q: How does feeding distance impact feeding of chicks?

A: Rearing chicks is a balancing act. The numbers of chicks that can be reared successfully must be balanced against: the amount of food that can be brought back (which in turn is determined by the distance that must be traveled to reach it and the time taken to catch it); the length of the breeding season (or the period over which an adequate food supply will be available); and the size of the chicks (which dictates how much food they will need). Inshore feeders typically attempt to rear two chicks. Offshore feeders, such as Magellanic, Chinstrap, and Adelie penguins, rear two chicks if conditions allow but the brood size tends to get reduced to one chick if they do not. Crested penguins, which feed even farther away from their colonies, lay two eggs

but only ever rear one chick. King and Emperor penguins, which travel farther again, and can be away from the nests for weeks at a time even during the chick-rearing stages, do not even bother trying to have two of their large chicks, opting instead for a single egg.

Q: Do other adults help feed the chicks?

A: Early penguin researchers, such as Dr. Murray Levick—who accompanied Captain Robert Falcon Scott on his ill-fated expedition to Antarctica in a bid to reach the South Pole—thought that penguin society was a lot less selfish than our own and that adults returning to the colony would feed any hungry chick. The consequences of Levick's mistakes were a lot less terminal than those of his leader, but the fact remains that failed breeders do not feed chicks and parents feed only their own chicks.

Q: How are chicks fed?

A: Parents must bring food back to their chicks and regurgitate it. Chicks beg by calling and vibrating their bill against the parent's bill, which helps induce the vomiting. A parent may throw up into its chick's mouth as many as 10 to 20 times in a feeding bout. When the chicks are young they are fed on the nest.

Mom and Dad take turns feeding the chicks. In crested penguins, although females are the sole providers of food for

A Magellanic Penguin feeds its chick over its shoulder. When the food supply is plentiful, Magellanics rear two chicks, but when conditions are less favorable they may rear only one.

often with several days between them.

When parents have a single chick it is relatively easy to regulate feeds: chick begs, parent vomits. If there are two chicks in a brood, however, it is not so easy for the parents to ensure that each chick gets its fair share of the pie, so to speak.

Left: An Adelie parent feeding its chick. Penguins must eat their catch and then regurgitate it into their chicks' mouths, sometimes with difficulty.

Below: A Chinstrap chick begs to be fed by calling and vibrating its bill against the parent's bill to induce vomiting.

the first two to three weeks while males guard the chicks, both sexes forage for the chicks in the postguard stage.

Q: How often are chicks fed?

A: Young chicks are fed small amounts frequently, perhaps every few hours. As the chicks get older, they are fed less often but in greater volume. During the guard stage, it is usual for the adults to relieve each other daily or thereabouts. Toward the end of the postguard period, feeding visits become more sporadic,

Feeding Chases

Q: How do parents distribute food when they have two chicks?

A: Basically, parents are unable to distinguish between their two chicks and, while the chicks are being guarded, it is a case of might is right: if there is a size difference between the chicks, the bigger of the two chicks will get access at the to their two chicks evenly: they stand with their flippers apart and feed the chicks over their shoulder, first to one side and then to the other, supposedly making it difficult for one chick to monopolize both feeding points. This compares to the more normal feeding posture employed by penguins, where they feed their chicks directly in front of them. In such circumstances, the bigger chick is able to reach across the little chick until it has had its fill.

Pygoscelid penguins go literally one step farther—well, a whole lot of steps actually: they run away from their chicks in order to feed them more fairly. While the chicks are being guarded the parents have no way of preventing a large chick from garnering more than its share of the resources. But once the chicks have been left in crèches, the parents adopt a new strategy. A parent returning from the sea with a belly full of food approaches the colony and usually goes back to the nest site, whereupon it calls to its chicks, which will come a-running from the crèche. At this point, instead of feeding them, the adult swivels around and runs away with its chicks in hot pursuit. This is known as a feeding chase (You might well ask, where do these penguin biologists get their names from?). It has the effect of distributing food to both chicks because, while a big one may get fed first, once it is satiated it does not

Penguins in the genus *Pygoscelis*, such as the Adelie, have solved the problem of food distribution between two chicks by adopting a strategy know as the feeding chase.

expense of its smaller sib. That is okay if there is enough food to go around and the differences in their body sizes are not too exaggerated so that the smallest can still get to eat something. In crested penguins, however, such sibling rivalry within broods inevitably leads to the starvation of the smaller chick.

It is said that Magellanic Penguins have developed a cool trick for counteracting sibling competition and distributing food

the chicks outside of the boundaries of the breeding groups and crèches from which they derive a measure of protection from Skuas and the like.

The only hope for the chicks of surviving and becoming breeders themselves is to get big and fat fast. Growth brings with it protection from the Skuas, too. So it seems that parents use feeding chases as a mechanism to deliver food efficiently to their chicks, weighing the short-term risk of Skua predation against the certainty of failure if their chicks are too small when they fledge.

The larger of two chicks can muscle out the smaller one, but as a consequence of the feeding chase, the smaller one will get its turn to gorge on regurgitated fish or krill.

run so energetically and this allows the little one to get to the regurgitated fish and krill first, or, as often happens, the chicks become separated (as a result of bumping into other chicks or adults and getting disorientated) and one or other of the chicks is able to feed untroubled by interference from its brother or sister.

It may seem extraordinary, chaotic, and too reliant on chance, but it really is effective at distributing the food more evenly between contesting chicks. When food supply is abundant, the chicks tend not to be so vigorous in their competition and feeding chases are much reduced. Similarly, parents with single chicks tend not to have very long feeding chases, if any at all. The big problem with feeding chases, however, is that they often take

In the case of only chicks, feeding chases tend to be short, if there are any at all.

Fledging

Q: What is fledging?

A: Fledging is that moment in a chick's life when it must say good-bye to room service and go out into the world to obtain its own food. It is the moment of independence. It is leaving home for good.

The age at which chicks fledge varies from species to species. The breeding season is shorter at high latitudes, but the compensation for this is a more pronounced food supply coupled with increased daylight during summer, which permits visual predators like penguins to feed around the clock in the deep south. Offshore feeders take advantage of these conditions, using their strategy of long periods at sea to enable them to get to the areas of high productivity and to convert that into chick mass. The critical determinant of whether chicks will make it on their own is their body mass at fledging.

An inshore-feeding strategy works best in tropical to subtropical areas where there is a more constant, less extreme food supply and the parents can take all the time in the world to rear their offspring. At higher latitudes, such an inshore-feeding strategy is not

A fledgling Little Penguin, replete with a topknot of remaining down and a white throat that marks it out from the black-throated adults.

as efficient at delivering food to chicks as is an offshore one: inshore feeders such as Gentoo and Yellow-eyed penguins take 89 and 106 days, respectively, to fatten their chicks to fledging, which is twice as long as comparably sized offshore feeders such as Adelie Penguins.

Q: When do chicks lose their down?

A: Before they can go to sea, chicks must get dressed properly: they undergo a molt, with their new feather survival suits growing and pushing out their down. There is a definite pattern to this down loss, or penguin pattern baldness: the down disappears first on the tummy and throat, then the back and, finally, the head. The last bit of down left is often a topknot, giving the chicks the appearance of having a punk-rock hairdo (Emperor Penguin chicks are different from all the rest: they fledge when they still have about 60 percent of their down).

In many instances, the plumage of fledglings is different from that of the adults: immature banded penguins do not have bands, immature crested penguins have pathetic little baby crests, while immature Adelie Penguins lack the black throat of their parents. By the time they turn up at the colonies as breeders, the immature birds will have molted into the complete adult uniform; they will have come of age. The general presumption has been that immature plumage inhibits or, at the very least, lessens the likelihood of being attacked by breeding-age birds.

Q: Do adult birds help the fledglings?

A: It is one of the great mysteries of life that juvenile seabirds seem to know what to do without practice or help. When it is time to leave, the chicks congregate at the water's edge. They may have a few false starts, where they dive in, splash wildly with their flippers, and then retreat to the shore. Eventually, however, they will just leave en masse, heading out to sea, calling excitedly to each other like school kids, their heads held above water like the new swimmers that they have just become. Confidence will come to them quickly. They will put their heads under, they will dive, they will truly have become like the fish they will need to catch to survive. They head off on a migration that will last a year and sometimes much more than that. Where they go and how they know how to get there remains a mystery.

Above: A band of fledgling Adelie Penguins gather at water's edge. Without practice or help, they will soon dive into the water and head out to sea.

Left: As a King chick matures, its down coat is replaced by a feather one. Penguins lose their down in a predictable pattern.

CHAPTER 8

BEHAVIOR

I f penguins could talk, you could imagine that the first words a fledgling chick might say when it takes its very first swim would be, "Whose idea was this?" Being a bird underwater must seem as alien as being a fish out of it.

Yet, although penguins cannot talk, communication is extremely important for them. In species where all the adults look alike and their kids do too, you might think that there would be the potential for huge mix-ups. But their voices and the way they use them are as individual for penguins as names are for us: penguins look alike, but they sound very different. At least to another penguin.

Above: Communication might seem to be problematic for bird species in which every individual looks just like its colony-mate.

Left: A Gentoo parent calls along with its neighbor as its chick rests atop its feet. Vocal communication is extremely important for penguins.

The other way penguins communicate is through posturing: the way they hold themselves can signal aggression, submission, that they are ready for sex, or dinner, or sleep. It may sound primitive, but think about how efficient we would be with our own communication if we did not have to interpret what someone said but could measure their thoughts by the way they held themselves. Actions really can speak louder than words, and they are much less likely to deceive.

Penguin Displays

Q: **What are the main types of penguin displays?**

A: People who study penguins are wont to describe their behavior. There is a problem, however, when it comes to comparing behaviors between the species—penguin biologists use different names to describe similar behaviors in different species. Another problem is that penguin biologists sometimes use emotive or suggestive names that imply a motivation for a behavior that may or may not be justified. Others have tried to get around this by using purely physical descriptors of behaviors, with a resulting set of unwieldy adjectives.

The main thing is that all penguins are derived from the same ancestors and, as a consequence, there is a commonality to much of their behavior that reflects descent from a common starting point. Penguin displays principally involve trumpeting calls, quivering, bowing, and shaking and swinging the head.

In all species the males have a display that is used to proclaim self, and to advertise their availability for females. It typically starts with the bird swinging its head from side to side or, perhaps, bowing toward its feet, and the display culminates with it pointing its bill skyward and letting out a long call. The flippers are held out and the head may or may not be moved from side to side. It has been called various things including vertical head swinging, braying, and the rather suggestive ecstatic display or ecstatic vocalization.

The other major display of penguins, which is also accompanied by calling, is the one used between pairs. Variations of it are used between a parent and chicks and, even, by an incubating adult to its eggs. The display typically involves facing the other individual and, in its most intense form, calling loudly to it. The two individuals may call together, waving their upturned heads about each other as they do so. There are also less intense, quieter versions. Mainly this behavior is used for individual recognition of partners, parents, and offspring. It typically occurs between mates when they are reunited at the start of the season and during nest

A male Magellanic Penguin lets out a long, braylike call. Variations of this display are common to males of all penguin species.

An isabelline Adelie and its partner bow to each other. Bowing, with the bills pointed downward, are nonthreatening displays that constitute penguin foreplay.

relief ceremonies. Incubating birds that have been on the nest for a long time will frequently stand and give such a call to their eggs. Adults brooding chicks will similarly call to them and, once they reach the postguard stage, the call is used to announce the parent's return from sea as well as to reinforce the bond between parent and chicks.

There are various other behaviors to do with their daily life. When wanting to make themselves nonthreatening to walk through the colony, say, penguins will sleek their feathers and walk on tippy-toes to make themselves appear slender and less threatening. In contrast, if they are being aggressive, they raise their crests (if they have one) and fluff their feathers. They use eye contact and stares to intimidate. It is all very stylized and gentle, like watching tiny sumo wrestlers go through their prefight rituals. Of course, if all that Tai Chi–like stuff fails to deter or defuse the situation, they can attack with bills at the ready. And they are especially good at meting out a flipper-bashing: rapid blows of their stiff flippers delivered with the staccato beat and tenderness of a Gatling gun.

When penguins become seductive they are more coy than brazen, more Maybe West than Mae West. Bowing is the rule, with males and females approaching each other in deep bows. Since their bills are their weapons, it is a way the males can show the females that they will not hurt them, like putting their pistols away.

Unusual Behaviors

Q: What is strange about the behavior of banded penguins?

A: Banded penguins, those penguins belonging to the genus *Spheniscus*—the Magellanic, Humboldt, African and Galápagos penguins— exhibit a behavior between pairs that involves dancing about each other, much like a tango, before clacking their bills together, making a sound reminiscent of castanets.

A pair of Humboldt Penguins engage in the slow tango that precedes bill duelling.

This behavior is called bill dueling. No other penguins do this, but, oddly, it is seen in albatross too. Is it possible the same behavior could have evolved twice, or does it more reasonably point to a common ancestry with albatross? While it certainly takes two to tango, some penguins demonstrate that it does not matter which two.

Q: Do male penguins engage in homosexual behavior?

A: As a group, males of any species are not a particularly discriminating lot. Biologically there are good reasons for this. They produce their gametes—their seeds, if you will—by the truckload. Well, maybe not quite that much, but a heck of a lot. In contrast, each breeding season a female penguin produces at most two eggs. Consequently, the eggs are much more valuable to the female than individual sperm is to the male. She needs to be careful that she does not waste her reproductive potential because she only gets the one shot. In contrast, the evolutionary costs to a male of making a mistake are much less expensive. Pumped up on testosterone at the start of the breeding season, males are likely to try to mate with anything. Something lying down and vaguely penguinlike is enough for them (scientists studying sperm competition take advantage of this by using the fluffy penguin toys one can buy in a shop as models to collect sperm), and it is not uncommon for males to mount an unsuspecting male having a siesta: there has even been a case of males taking turns to mount each other. So, maybe homosexual behavior among penguins is less about mistaken identity and more a case of practice makes perfect?

The female penguins, too, are not without their vices.

Q: Is it true that female penguins engage in prostitution?

A: When a female Adelie Penguin completes laying and her male partner is sitting on the eggs, she will go to look for stones to shore up the sides of their nest. She will soon be heading out to sea and leaving the male sitting tight on the eggs for a couple of weeks or more. Stones are used to line the nest and help keep the eggs free of any meltwater. Usually females search for stones on the ground outside their subcolony if they are industrious, or steal them from neighbors' nests if they are a bit devious; however, some females have learned to exploit the fact that unpaired males think more with their cloacas than they do with their heads.

Males that have been unsuccessful at attracting a mate are typically young and have a nest site on the periphery of the breeding group. Without any of the normal domestic duties that consume paired penguins, the males are free to go on a stone-collecting extravaganza: these unpaired males often have nests made with so many stones that they look like small castles. Females that have completed laying and are in need of stones sometimes approach these males in a deep bow as if they want to have sex with them. The males bow back, then, as is normal, step aside to let the female lie down in the nest. What is not normal is that the female will move onto the nest, choose a stone, then hightail it back to her own nest. The duped males are so stupid, or eager, or both, that it is not uncommon for the female to repeat the performance, as many as twenty times in some instances.

It could be argued that the Adelie males have nothing to lose but their dignity (and let's face it, how much dignity can males that will mount a toy penguin have?), but occasionally, just occasionally, the females will have sex with the males before taking a stone. Prostitution? Maybe. A cunning way of collecting stones? Definitely.

When in need of stones to shore up their nests, female Adelies may trick unpaired males into thinking that they will have sex with them. Instead of mating, however, the female moves onto the nest, grabs a stone, and then dashes back to her own nest.

> Penguins mate for life. That doesn't surprise me much because they all look alike. It's not like they're going to meet a really new, great-looking penguin someday.
>
> —ANONYMOUS

Alternative Breeding Strategies

In order to complete breeding within one year, the large Emperor Penguins must incubate their single eggs during the frightfully cold Antarctic winter so that the arrival of chicks coincides with the availability of plentiful food in spring and summer.

Q: Why do Emperor Penguins do things differently than other breeding penguins?

A: The Emperor Penguin has just about the most unenviable system of reproduction of any animal. Emperor Penguins confound logic in that they breed during the heart of the Antarctic winter. But really, when you think about it, all they are doing is responding to what is possible now that penguins have become flightless wannabe fish. Their survival suit of feathers for being in water allowed them to be comfortable out of it in the cold; and their large size—possible once they no longer needed to fly—meant that they could reduce their surface area relative to their volume, enhancing their ability to withstand cold even further. So, just when other animals are shutting up shop, getting on their migratory bikes and getting the heck out of Antarctica, the emperors head south in March and April and form colonies on the surface of the sea, which by then has frozen solid.

There is no way that parents could raise more than one large offspring and so, by reducing the clutch size to one egg, they are able to carry it on their feet (walking with two eggs, on the other hand, would be a recipe for scrambled eggs), which frees them from the need to build and maintain nest sites. This permits Emperors to breed on ice. The enormous size of the males, especially, enables them to go for more than a quarter of the year without eating. And because they can be mobile with the egg, they can huddle together during the dark Antarctic winter when the temperature does not so much drop below freezing as it free-falls. The esophageal milk produced by males gives them some leeway should the females be late returning with food when the chicks hatch. Hatching coincides with the start of the spring bloom and the period of high Antarctic productivity.

When you think about it, because they are so large and have such a large egg that takes such a long time to develop, if

Emperors started breeding in spring with everyone else, by the time their chicks hatched and needed food there would be hardly any left. The bloom would have bloomed; the spring would have long since ris'. So really, Emperors had no choice but to start early, to start their breeding season in the beginning of winter. Even then, by the time the ice on which they breed breaks up, the chicks will not yet have reached adult size. At the time of fledging, Emperor Penguin chicks are still largely covered with down: they fledge in a developmentally premature state compared to other penguins. The chicks are left to fend for themselves at the height of Antarctica's productivity and to finish off a job that their parents started.

If you are a big flightless penguin and need to produce an equally big but helpless chick, it is not easy to complete breeding within one year. King Penguins do not even try.

Q: How do King Penguins breed?

A: King Penguins have many of the attributes of their cousins the Emperors: they are big and they lay a single egg that they carry on their feet. Where they differ

is that when it comes to breeding on their subantarctic islands, they do not even attempt to get from go to whoa in less than a year: they take 14 to 16 months to fledge their chicks. This means that, unusually for birds, rather than breeding annually, they breed twice every three years. At any one time in a King Penguin colony, then, there will be two quite distinct cohorts of young: some adults may be incubating eggs while some may be feeding large chicks.

The really remarkable thing about King Penguins, and it is perhaps the most remarkable thing about all penguins, is that over the winter period chicks are left on their own while the adults travel hundreds, even thousands, of miles to find food, leaving the chicks to starve for months at a time. In the most extreme cases, chicks can go five and a half months without food, which is a long time between feeds in anyone's book. At least the King Penguin chicks have parents that feed them eventually.

Left: Like their cousins the Emperors, King Penguins lay a single egg that they carry on their feet. Unlike Emperors, however, they take more than a year to fledge their chicks.

Below: At any one time in a King Penguin colony there are likely to be two cohorts: some adults may be incubating eggs while others are looking after large chicks.

Brood Reduction

Q: Why would a penguin lay two eggs if it can only ever rear one chick?

A: It remains one of biology's greatest mysteries: crested penguins—those of the crazy eyebrows—are described, with

A Macaroni Penguin incubates an egg: the real mystery is why it bothered to lay two.

all the romance that only a biologist can muster, as obligate brood reducers. What this means in practice is that they lay two eggs, but only ever successfully rear one of them to fledging. It is not as wacky as it may sound on the surface, and some birds of prey and seabirds, such as Skuas and boobies, adopt similar strategies. In those instances, however, it is fairly clear that the extra egg functions as a form of insurance against loss of the first. Put another way, given that the birds are capable of rearing only one offspring, those that lay two eggs are more likely to produce that one offspring than those that lay only a

single egg because, if the latter lose their egg or chick, they have no other options.

Crested penguins do not fit that mold, however. Among the five species there is variation in when the brood reduction typically occurs. In Macaroni and Erect-crested penguins the first-laid egg is usually lost before or on the day the second is laid: the equivalent of taking out an insurance policy and then tearing it up. And notice something else: it is the first-laid egg that is lost. Similarly, for the other crested penguin species, it is usually the first-laid egg or the chick from the first-laid egg that dies. The poorer prospects of the first-laid egg have led the crested penguins to reduce investment in it, making it much smaller than the second-laid egg; what is known as intraclutch egg-size dimorphism. Erect-crested Penguins have the most extreme egg-size differences of any birds, with the second egg being about 85 percent larger than the first.

Despite the second egg being laid four or five days after the first egg, it is the chick from the second-laid egg that hatches first in those species where both chicks tend to hatch. The larger second egg has more albumin, with proteins that promote growth, and is incubated in the more favorable posterior position beneath the brood patch. In such species (Snares, Fiordland, and Rockhopper), death of the smaller second-hatched chick (which comes from the smaller first-laid egg) usually occurs within the first 12 days, long before the feeding demands of the chicks are sufficient to strain the ability of the parents to provide for both of them.

In a great many birds, an optional form of brood reduction may occur, which, according to the theory of ornithologist David Lack (1910–73), allows birds to adjust their brood size to the prevailing food supply. But in the case of the crested penguins, there is nothing optional about it, no adjusting to the current conditions; reduction occurs regardless of conditions (there have only ever been one or two isolated reports of parents rearing two chicks).

What seems apparent is that crested penguins feed so far offshore that logistically they simply cannot transport enough food back over such distances to feed two chicks.

Q: **Why then do crested penguins not just lay just one egg?**

A: There is no really satisfactory answer to this yet. These birds were probably derived from ancestors not dissimilar to Yellow-eyed Penguins, which lay two similar-sized eggs. In the course of their evolutionary history, for whatever reason, second eggs proved more likely to produce surviving offspring and, as a consequence, natural selection encouraged parents to put more of their food basket in that egg, making it bigger. If—and this is pure speculation—it subsequently became advantageous to have only a single egg, they may not have been able to simply stop laying the unwanted first egg. They could put as little albumin in it as they liked, they could ignore it when it was laid, but the first egg would still have remained a necessary precursor, biologically, for the development of the favored second egg. Who knows? It is just one of the many mysteries about crested penguins.

Left: The smaller first-laid eggs of crested penguins, such as those of Erect-crested Penguins, are usually lost by the time the second one is laid.

Below: Rockhopper Penguins, even though they may manage to hatch two chicks, as do other crested penguins, only rear a single chick to fledging.

Bullying Behavior

Q: Why are the crested penguins such bullies?

A: Crested penguins are different from other penguins on a number of fronts. One of the most obvious is that after the female has laid both eggs, instead of one of the parents rushing off to sea to replenish its fat reserves exhausted by the weeks onshore for courtship and egg-laying,

A study of Erect-crested Penguins showed that males remained with the female for up 13 days and for as little as 2 days, depending upon when they finished laying, with males from clutches laid last staying for the least amount of time. What this meant was that the colony did not empty itself of males piecemeal as clutches were completed, but rather all at once: in just three days all the breeding

A pair of male Erect-crested Penguins bully a female left to incubate after her partner left her to go to sea.

both parents continue to stay together at the nest. This is strange because only one of them is able to incubate the eggs at a time and it would seem to make no sense for the male to hang around for longer than he has to (in all but the Fiordland species, it is the male that will eventually go to sea first).

males left to go to sea. Then something happened that merely confirmed that crested penguins are the weirdos of the whole bird world: nonbreeding birds, often operating in pairs, attacked the females left sitting on the nests.

This bullying behavior usually takes the form of the aggressive penguins pecking the defenseless female while she is lying down and bashing her with their flippers. Attacks can last for a few seconds, but are often repeated and, in sustained cases, may last for up to an hour. The victim's response to all of this is to assume the braced position—a sort of penguin in-fight safety tip—with her flippers spread-eagled and her face turned down into the ground, eyes closed, protecting her clutch and herself as best she can. Sometimes the beatings meted out are so severe that the female cannot stand it and is driven off the nest. Her one or two eggs as good as dead; it is just a matter of time before they are broken.

In Snares Penguins, where this behavior has also been studied, it is the small first-laid egg that is the most likely to be broken, whether the female is driven off the nest or not. In the case of the Snares

Penguins, the bullies were not just the unemployed louts loitering around the colony after the real lads had gone, but were often also breeding males from neighboring nests. In other words, by leaving first, males expose their females to bullying. This might well explain why male crested penguins do not rush off to sea at the first opportunity. As long as their stomachs will allow, they continue to stay as a form of mate guarding, or, more correctly, egg guarding. But none of that can explain why crested penguins, male or female, should bully in the first place. What advantage—and we are talking evolutionary advantage here—can there be to performing such behavior? The scientists are still scratching their heads.

Alice's comment in Lewis Carroll's *Through the Looking Glass* best sums up crested penguins: "Curioser and curioser." Indeed.

Above: Underscoring just how peculiar crested penguins can be, a Rockhopper male attempts to pair up with an Erect-crested female.

Left: A battered female Erect-crested Penguin after being driven from her nest by a pair of bullies.

CHAPTER 9

MOLT

"A long time between feeds," is how an adult penguin might well describe molt, for it is arguably the most grueling, energy-sapping thing penguins do. Even if their eggs did not tie penguins to the land, that other characteristic that so defines them as birds, most surely would. Feathers provide the insulation that allows penguins to immerse themselves in water and still maintain the warm body temperatures that their metabolisms demand. Feathers allow them to walk on land in places so cold that others fear to tippy-toe, let alone to tread. Feathers are fantastic. But there is one downside to feathers: they wear out. They lose their effectiveness. They lose their insulative abilities.

Above: It is their feather survival suits that allow penguins, such as this Gentoo, to immerse themselves for long periods in water.

Left: Out with the old and in with the new: a Snares Penguin molts.

Changing a feather coat is not as simple as taking one off and slipping into another. It is a slow process whereby new feathers must be manufactured and grow, pushing out the old feathers as they do. And the irony is that this process of renewal is itself debilitating: while molting, penguins are at their most vulnerable. They are robbed of much of their insulation. They cannot go to sea. They cannot eat. Yet, it is energetically taxing. So, they must stand, immobile, trying to conserve what energy they can for the process of making new feathers.

Feathers

Q: What are feathers?

A: Feathers are one of those things that most people think they know what they are. They are distinct and relatively easy to describe: the filamentous structures that cover birds. But in reality, it is harder to describe them exactly and even harder to know exactly what they are. They are outgrowths of the epidermis—or skin, for want of a simpler word—made up largely of proteins called keratin, with water (8 percent) and a tiny amount of fat (1 percent) making up the rest. Keratin is the same substance that in humans forms fingernails and hair. In fact, feathers grow from follicles or pits in the skin, much as our hair does.

Q: How did feathers evolve?

A: Feathers are thought to have evolved from the scales of reptilian ancestors and, while some are now questioning this theory, it seems most likely that they did. Although all birds have feathers—and they remain a defining characteristic of birds—in the last ten years, some ancient dinosaur fossils have been discovered with feathers, too. These have come especially from 124-million-year-old deposits around Liaoning, China. This is the same area in which one of science's most famous hoaxes was perpetrated: in 1999, *National Geographic* magazine announced to the world that a new fossil, christened *Archaeoraptor*, was the missing link between dinosaurs and birds. It turned out that they had been duped: a Chinese farmer had created the fossil by gluing together fragments from two different fossils. *National Geographic* was forced to print a retraction. Despite that hoax, however, one thing science has managed to clarify in recent times is that birds are really just a group of dinosaurs that did not happen to get wiped out at the end of the Cretaceous. The occurrence of feathers in dinosaurs with lineages stretching back millions of years before birds took their first test flight, suggests that feathers evolved for something other than flight. The most often cited reason is for insulation: feathers could prevent an animal from getting too cold or too hot.

Of course, that is all fine and dandy on land. If you have ever slept in a down sleeping bag or under a feather duvet, you will know how efficient they can

A Little Penguin has 300 to 400 percent more feathers than an equivalently sized flying bird.

be at keeping out the cold. The loft of the filaments of the down and feathers traps a layer of air. Sleep out in the rain in a down sleeping bag, however, and you will have a most uncomfortable and cold night. Down and feathers lose their loft—the air-filled spaces—when soaking wet and, with it, their insulative abilities. It is one reason why sleeping bags with synthetic fills, which maintain their loft when wet, are popular with climbers and adventurers who must endure damp conditions.

On the surface, then, it would seem unlikely that feathers should be used for insulating an aquatic creature.

Without the insulation provided by their feathers, Adelie Penguins are forced to remain on land throughout the molt.

Penguins and Molt

Q: How can feathers keep penguins warm in water?

A: In flying birds, the contour feathers that cover most of the body are arranged in tracts. In contrast, the contour feathers of penguins are distributed uniformly across the whole body and at much higher densities. Penguins have 300 to 400 percent more feathers than equivalently sized flying birds. The shafts of the feathers are flattened, curved, and lie along the penguin's body, providing a mechanical framework for the rest of the feather. Muscles at the base of the feathers enable them to be raised and lowered like louvers when on land, thereby allowing airflow to move in or out, helping to control temperatures by such venting. Penguin feathers are typically short—about one and a half inches (30–40 mm) long—and stiff. The barbs, which are arranged as branches on either side of the shaft and together form the vane, have hooks—known as barbules—which lock together, creating a rigid watertight covering. It is for this reason that the feathers of penguins are nothing like the fluffy coverings of toy penguins: they are coarse. Run your hand down a penguin's back and it will glide smoothly over the surface, but run it back "against the grain" and it will feel rough and prickly, like running your hand up against Velcro the wrong way. In fact, the analogy with Velcro is an apt one: when the barbules are hooked together, they provide a strong bond, similar to the way the hooks and loops of Velcro lock together.

Near the base of the feathers are long downy filaments, which are without barbules. These trap the air and give it the loft necessary to insulate the skin, whereas the highly dense, interlocked, evenly distributed main parts of the feathers stop water seeping through to the skin. They resist compression when the penguin dives so that much of the trapped air is prevented from escaping. Watch video footage of penguins diving underwater and you will see streams of bubbles left in their wake as they dive down; but what you cannot see is that much of the air remains trapped between the skin and the interlocked feathers.

With such a system of insulation crucial for penguins to survive for long periods in the sea—their source of sustenance—there is probably no really good time to have to give it up, but give it up they must.

Although penguins appear to be made of fluff, their feathers are actually rough and prickly.

Q: When do penguins molt?

A: Most penguins molt after they have completed breeding. The exceptions are some of the *Spheniscus* (banded)

penguins and King Penguins: Galápagos and Humboldt penguins tend to molt before breeding, while African Penguins can molt either before or after breeding, as can the Kings. For the Galápagos, Humboldt, and African penguins, which are the penguin species that breed closest to the equator, it becomes a bit academic as to just what constitutes "before" and what constitutes "after" breeding because, if conditions are favorable, breeding can occur during any month of the year and they may attempt to breed more than once per year. Likewise, King Penguins, with their more-than-a-year breeding cycle, either molt before or after breeding, depending upon where they are when between cycles in relation to the time of year.

The main point is not so much *when* molt occurs, but that it *must* occur and that it requires heaps of energy. To sustain themselves through it, the penguins must be in peak condition, which means going on a feeding binge of impressive proportions.

Ironically, the process of molting, which ultimately enables penguins to go to sea, is itself debilitating, leaving these Chinstrap Penguins to gaze at the ocean: more "see" birds than seabirds.

Pre-molt

Q: **What is the pre-molt feeding trip?**

A: Exhausted by the effort of trying to rear their chicks, most penguins discover that they have undergone a

Snares Penguins undergo long feeding trips at sea to fatten up before returning to land to molt.

drastic diet. The burden of parenthood is likely to have shed up to one-third or more of their body weight. To regain condition, penguins embark on a feeding extravaganza, spending weeks at sea stuffing their faces with a never-ending sushi salad. The pre-molt feeding trip can vary from less than two weeks—in the case of Antarctic breeding penguins, such as Adelies, where the last flush of the summer blooms mean that food can still be found in abundance—to up to ten weeks in the case of some of the crested

species such as Fiordland and Snares. The exact timing of the pre-molt feeding trip is highly constrained and synchronous in the offshore-feeding penguins of the higher latitudes. By contrast, in the lower latitudes, the inshore-feeding species are variable in both the timing and duration of the pre-molt feeding trip, suggesting that it is determined by local food availability, which tends to be less predictable than the highly seasonal pattern of food availability farther south.

Q: **Where do penguins go on their pre-molt feeding trips?**

A: This is a question in search of a 64-million-dollar answer. Well, maybe not that much, but certainly the answer will require investing thousands of dollars to track penguins at sea using various forms of telemetry and data loggers. There has been little work done on tracking penguins during this stage of their life cycles simply because, in contrast to breeding birds that return to a fixed and known nest site, penguins on pre-molt foraging trips do not generally return to their actual nests. This increases the risk of being unable to retrieve expensive tracking equipment, especially as the process of molt means that any device attached to the feathers will fall off (and potentially be lost forever) if the researchers do not get to the penguin first.

Q: Where do penguins molt?

A: Although they don't necessarily return to their nest sites, most penguins return to the general vicinity of their colonies to molt. They often stand in the lee of cliffs to find shelter from wind or down near the water's edge, looking as disheveled as any hobos. Adelie Penguins, however, for the most part do not molt back at their colonies but do so while drifting around the Antarctic seas on pieces of pack ice. That is one advantage of breeding in the Antarctic: why travel all the way back to solid ground if you can stay dry and out of the water by standing on it?

Adelie Penguins tend not to molt on their nest site or, even, their colony.

The Process of Molting

Q: What happens during molt?

A: Molt is the process whereby penguins discard their survival suit of feathers in favor of a new season's model. They do this by essentially letting the new feathers grow beneath the old ones, pushing them out. This enables them to have partial, if not very effective, insulation. Think of swapping a down jacket for a T-shirt: the latter is better than nothing, but that is about all you can say for it. As the displaced feathers are pushed out, they lose their connectivity to each other, which means that a layer of air cannot be trapped effectively against the skin. And, when the old feathers fall out, the new ones are too short to provide really effective insulation until they grow longer. To minimize the period over which they are vulnerable to the cold, penguins molt all their feathers at once. The downside to this extreme makeover, doing everything at once, is that it places a great energetic strain on their bodies to produce the necessary proteins to make the feathers.

And the catch-22 in all of this is that the penguins cannot go to sea to feed to get the energy for molting because, of course, the process of molting robs them of the necessary insulation to forage at sea. As a consequence, they must fast throughout the entire molt, which typically takes two to five weeks. Even inshore feeders, not used to stints on the nest of more than a day or two, must be capable of fasting for a period of weeks.

What a fast it is, too. When incubating their eggs, penguins minimize movement and energy utilization, relying largely on their fat stores to provide for their energetic needs. If fat levels reduce to the point where the penguins must start burning appreciable amounts of protein to meet their energy budget, they will abandon the eggs to search for food. For molting penguins, it is essential that they conserve energy too while fasting and living off fat accumulated during the pre-molt period of gluttony,

Penguins molt all of their feathers simultaneously, although there tends to be a pattern in which the old feathers fall out, with those on the tummy usually being among the first to go, such as on this African Penguin.

A King Penguin conserves
energy while molting by
lying down on the job.

but—and it is a big but—they must
also manufacture the protein for their
feathers. Although the amino acids used
to make the feather proteins are derived
largely from fat, up to 15 percent of the
energy required for molt must come from
proteins used in the manufacture of the
new feathers. At least that is the case for
King Penguins, the species in which molt
has been studied most extensively. And
the source of that protein, then? The birds'
own muscles. Little wonder then that
molting is the time when adult penguins
are at their most vulnerable. Little
wonder then that they stack on as much
body mass as they can beforehand. Little
wonder then that they bulk their muscles
up like body builders on steroids.

Adult penguins are at their heaviest
just prior to molt, even more so than at
the start of the breeding season. Breast
and leg muscles expand like some avian
imitation of Arnold Schwarzenegger.
A King Penguin that weighs 35 pounds
(16 kg) at its waddling best at the start of
the breeding season, will somehow manage to top the scales at 40 pounds (18 kg)
before starting molt. Even so, in times of
poor food supply some penguins do not
survive the process of molting: it is such a
touch-and-go enterprise, such a drain on
their internal resources, that by the time
the molt has ended the penguin will have
lost well over half its body weight.

If penguins have a motto, it must surely
be: *live for today, but eat for tomorrow.*

**An Emperor penguin was found on the Cape
well advanced in moult, a good specimen skin.**
—*Robert Falcon Scott*

The Completion of Molt

Q: What are the phases of molt?

A: The molt has three recognized phases to it. Manufacture of the new feathers actually begins while the penguins are still at sea on their pre-molt feeding trip. During the first phase, after they have come ashore, the penguins reduce their metabolic rate, which really means that they reduce the amount of energy they are consuming by not doing anything more strenuous than standing or yawning. The second phase is the long period of steady depletion of their fat reserves as they continue to do as little as possible while persevering with making their feathers. Even while standing still, however, these guys use up energy faster than a V8 pickup truck at traffic lights. Rates of energy consumption are half as much again as when they are incubating eggs, principally because they are not insulated as well, requiring them to burn more fat to stay warm, and also because they must use energy to produce their feathers. The molting penguins may or may not get to the third phase, which is the most dangerous, because this is when the fat reserves are nearly exhausted and the birds are forced to complete the process by consuming the proteins in their muscles.

The time to complete molt is variable and can depend on the environmental conditions. When the weather conditions are unfavorable, the penguins must devote more energy to simply staying warm and this slows their completion of the molt because it takes them longer to manufacture their feathers.

Q: What role might carotenoid pigments play?

A: Penguins never look better dressed than just after they have molted. Their feathers are sleek, almost shiny. In some penguins, notably the crested penguins, Yellow-eyed, King, and Emperor penguins, there are flashes of color that offset their black-and-white attire: a yellow crest here, an orange cheek pad there. The function of such conspicuous ornamental traits is not exactly clear. They apparently have a role in species recognition: females will typically mate only with males exhibiting the ornamental characteristics peculiar to their species. For a Yellow-eyed Penguin that might be the

The orange feathers of King Penguins are produced by depositing carotenoid pigments in them: these pigments cannot be produced by the penguins and must be obtained from their diet.

band of yellow feathers around the head. For a Rockhopper Penguin it may be the yellow crests that droop down the sides of the face. For a King Penguin it may be the orange cheeks. This is not something peculiar to such penguins, as the purely black-and-white penguins surely utilize other characteristics for species recognition, such as the white eye ring in Adelies. But yellows, oranges, and reds in bird plumage are made by pigments called carotenoids that are deposited in the feathers. The interesting thing is that carotenoids cannot be manufactured by birds; they must be obtained through their diet. There is, therefore, a growing interest in whether the amount of carotenoids deposited in feathers could be used as a marker for the quality of a bird, a sort of diagnostic gauge of their potential worth. In the same way that we may look at someone driving a Porsche and presume that they are rich, scientists are wondering whether female birds, especially, can use such things as the amount of red, orange, or yellow in a prospective mates' plumage to indicate whether they are likely to be good providers.

It is controversial as to what relevance this might have for penguins, but preliminary work indicates that male Yellow-eyed Penguins in the best condition have yellow feathers that are more highly saturated (in other words, they would look more yellow to us). This raises the possibility, then, that female Yellow-eyed Penguins could potentially choose better-quality partners based upon how yellow their feathers are, which at the very least should be an

indicator of how well the bird can forage. That is the theory, but there is many a good theory that has come unstuck as fast as the feathers from a molting penguin once more evidence is available. At this stage, it is like looking into the unknown, which is how, indeed, most penguins would feel if they could contemplate the next major challenge in their lives: migration.

Once they are decked out in their shiny new suits, penguins such as this Chinstrap are free to head back to the water.

CHAPTER 10

MIGRATION

If having to go through the energetically draining process of changing their clothes was not bad enough for penguins that had just completed the exhausting job of bringing new life into the world, many of them have to pack up their bags and move to a new location in the off-season. This is especially so for the offshore feeders that nest mainly at high latitudes. At the end of the breeding season, conditions start to deteriorate: the weather and, particularly, the food supply.

For young and old penguins alike, migration is the most dangerous time of their lives. Many do not make it back to their colonies to breed. Swimming is a costly exercise. On the other flipper, this is also the period when penguins are at their most liberated, the period when they are not tied to the land by the twin necessities of breeding and molting, the period when they really can be like fish.

For fledgling penguins, migration is a rite of passage: the journey from chick to penguinhood. For adult penguins, despite the miles upon exhausting miles traveled, it is strangely about marking time, standing still, getting ready to have the next big crack at breeding. From an evolutionary point of view, such a holiday at sea would not be tolerated unless it somehow helped parents to have more babies.

Above: An African Penguin takes to the water. Typically nonmigratory, it possesses the same navigational abilities as do the migratory species of penguins.

Left: Penguin tracks: the beginning and end of migration takes place on land for all penguins except the Emperor.

Reasons for Migration

Q: Why do penguins migrate?

A: In the higher latitudes, the seasons are more pronounced. With the shortening of the day length as winter approaches, there is less photosynthesis (in the case of the marine environment, this means fewer phytoplankton) and less basis for life. In the farthest reaches, ice and snow may cover both the sea and the land, rendering them inhospitable for any penguin, indeed anything, not called an Emperor. But it is largely the drastic reduction in the available food supply that dictates penguins at high latitudes must head north for the winter. Of course, there is another way to look at this: that is, the brief but highly productive growing season found in the summer at high latitudes is what attracts penguins to head there for breeding. Like their flying ancestors, where flight gave them the opportunity to exploit environments that could not support life all year round, migration, even by swimming, means that penguins can take advantage of the good times elsewhere. But swimming is not an easy way to get around.

Q: Do all penguins migrate?

A: Migration is so costly, both in energetic terms and in terms of its attendant dangers, that it is easy to imagine that where conditions permit penguins to stay resident, they should be in no great hurry to leave. Gentoo Penguins probably illustrate this notion better than any other species. There are two subspecies of Gentoos: a northern subspecies that

The conditions at higher latitudes, such as the Antarctic, force penguins to abandon the place during winter, except for Emperor Penguins, which although migratory, return to the Antarctic at the start of winter to begin the process of breeding.

nests on subantarctic islands—such as the Falklands, Marion, and Crozet islands—and a southern subspecies that nests on the Antarctic Peninsula. Gentoos are inshore feeders and the northern forms tend to remain resident around their colonies for the entire year. In the Antarctic, conditions deteriorate to such an extent that they are forced to migrate away for a few months; much shorter than the migrations of their offshore-feeding neighbors, the Adelie and Chinstrap Penguins, but nevertheless, in the Antarctic, Gentoos cannot stay the course. Similarly, the inshore-feeding Humboldt Penguins on the coast of Peru and northern Chile remain resident year-round. But in some years, El Niño so depletes the local food supply that they have been recorded as migrating nearly six hundred miles to find an area with more food.

Gentoo Penguins breeding at Cuverville Island, Antarctica, are migratory in contrast to their non-migratory fellow Gentoos breeding farther north.

Q: How did migration in penguins arise?

A: Although it is conjecture, and there is some conflicting evidence, logic suggests that flightless penguins initially arose as inshore-feeding residents inhabiting the warm waters that characterized the southern regions 60 million years ago. The issue for the inshore feeders is that the food supply, while available all year round, is of a relatively low density and this limits the pace at which, for want of a better way of putting it, food can be converted into chicks. In contrast, the highly productive waters that emerged in the colder southern seas with the formation of the circumpolar current, meant that penguins that bred there could convert food into chick mass at a higher rate than their more equatorial cousins. The price they paid for this expediency was that they had to move elsewhere come winter. From an evolutionary point of view, both strategies have their advantages: interestingly, in areas where residential inshore-feeding penguins and offshore-feeding migratory penguins overlap, the offshore feeders are able to fledge their chicks much more quickly. This might suggest that selection will promote such a strategy where conditions allow, as the higher productivity can outweigh the costs of migration.

Technology

Q: **How can researchers follow penguins at sea?**

A: In the last quarter century there has been a revolution in the study of penguins. Prior to 1980, the penguins we knew were the penguins of the land. They were the penguins ashore breeding, because they were the only penguins we could see. Yet penguins spend as much as 80 percent of their lives at sea. They are more deserving of the moniker "seabird" than any other group of birds. It was impossible to follow them in the water, however, and especially so during the long winter months, often spent in such inhospitable places as the Antarctic and the subantarctic.

It was the miniaturization of electronics that eventually exposed the wet side of the lives of penguins. Radio transmitters small enough to attach to penguins were developed. Admittedly, before this there had been attempts to track penguins—which look farcical now—with the penguins dressed in yellow waistcoats and enough weight to drown an elephant. In the early 1980s, scientists realized that the best way to attach devices to penguins was to glue them directly to the feathers, removing the need for any awkward attachments such as waistcoats, belts, or buckles and, by imbedding the devices in the feathers so that the feathers overlapped the front ends, this made them quite streamlined. A downside of this gluing, however, was that when the device was retrieved, the feathers had to be cut, essentially creating a puncture in their feather survival suits that must have let in water and cold to some extent. Later it was found that by using Tesa tape, a waterproof variety, the devices could be reliably taped to the feathers and, when it came time to retrieve the devices, they could then be simply unwrapped, leaving the

The first attempts to track penguins were admirable in their intentions but ludicrously compromised in retrospect: this Gentoo Penguin in its yellow waistcoat is more Sherpa than research subject.

feathers intact. This was much better for the penguins, but there were still other lessons to be learned.

Q: Does attaching devices to penguins affect their streamlining?

A: A penguin's body is so streamlined that any obstacle stuck onto it creates drag, disturbing the flow of water. Devices used to locate penguins at sea need either to transmit a signal to receiving antennae or communicate with orbiting satellites. This can only occur when the device is free of the water, which only happens when the penguin is on the surface (or out of the water). To maximize the chances of the aerial poking out of the water, researchers, naturally enough, placed the devices at the highest point on the center of the penguins' backs. The problem was that this also maximized the effects of drag. Although it is likely that penguins can compensate to some extent for the increased drag, initial studies showed that penguins used a worryingly high amount of extra energy to do so and there was always the concern that their behavior may have been altered, too: How could you know that a penguin with a device was going to the same places and following the same diving and resting patterns as a normal bird if it was being energetically stressed by the need to carry the extra hydrodynamic load that the devices imposed? Research in wind and water tunnels revealed that normal penguins not only had

abnormally low coefficients of drag but that by placing any device near the tail region of the back and tapering it so that the cross-sectional area at its front was reduced, like the nose of a formula one car, the effects of device attachment could be minimized.

There are essentially three basic types of attachments: radiotelemetry, satellite telemetry, and data logger.

Above: Much of the early work on diving and monitoring the at-sea behavior of penguins was conducted on the banded penguins; that is, those belonging to the genus *Spheniscus*.

Left: In contrast to the cumbersome attachments used to track the Gentoo Penguin on the opposite page, modern transmitters capable of communicating with satellites are small, streamlined and taped directly to the feathers on the lower part of the back.

Telemetry and Penguins

Q: How can radiotelemetry be used to track penguins at sea?

A: Radiotelemetry sends a signal from the device attached to the penguin to a receiving antenna, which can be land based or attached to aircraft such as fixed-wing planes or helicopters. Turning the antenna and taking a compass bearing at the point when the signal is

Radiotelemetry has long been used by biologists to track land-based birds, but its application to tracking penguins at sea posed new difficulties that needed to be surmounted by using aircraft or triangulation from twin towers.

strongest is used to derive the direction the animal is from the receiving antenna. All good stuff if all you want to know is that your penguin is, say, northwest of the colony. To work out actual locations you need to triangulate, which means taking bearings simultaneously from two different antennae and working out where the direction lines intersect. The ability to do this, and its accuracy, will depend in part on how far apart you have the two receiving antennae. But

the real downer is that the radio signals must be virtually "line of sight," which means that how far you can "see" with radiotelemetry out into the ocean will be dictated by how high you can get the receiving antennae and, even then, the curvature of the earth is likely to foil you from getting locations much more than 40 miles away. Which makes radiotelemetry fine for plotting the movements of inshore-feeding penguins that do not wander too far from their colonies, but useless for following the at-sea travels of offshore-feeding penguins when they travel beyond the radio horizon.

Q: How can satellite telemetry be used to track penguins at sea?

A: An alternative to radiotelemetry is to use satellite telemetry. In this case, the signal is transmitted not to a land-based tower but to a satellite orbiting above the atmosphere. The satellite, as it passes over the transmitter, will pick up a series of signals from it. Computers work out the location not using triangulation but by utilizing something known as the Doppler effect. This involves solving some equations that would make even Einstein's brain hurt, taking into account the time taken for the signal to reach the satellite as the satellite passes over that part of the Earth at a known altitude and speed. This method of calculating locations can be surprisingly accurate (within a mile or so), but its accuracy is affected by the number of signals the satellite receives and this is in turn affected by how much time the penguin spends at the surface. The other big downside, performance-wise, to satellite telemetry was that the battery power needed to send a signal that far meant that early versions of satellite transmitters were necessarily quite large. Advances in battery technology have reduced the size of satellite telemetry transmitters considerably. Even so, cost remains a formidable obstacle: typically it costs more to pay to access the data from the orbiting satellites than it does to buy the transmitters themselves, and at several thousand dollars each, they are not cheap. It can be a weird sensation to watch a penguin go to sea with electronics worth the price of a small car on its back, not knowing if you will ever see them again. But the great thing about satellite telemetry is that you at least get the data, even if you do not see the bird again or retrieve the device.

Above: The advantage of using satellites to track penguins is that they can potentially locate penguins anywhere on the globe with great accuracy. The disadvantage is that they cost a lot and the batteries needed to power the signal transmission limits how small they can be.

Left: A freshly molted Adelie Penguin with a satellite transmitter taped to its lower back just before embarking on its migration.

Data Loggers and Distances

Q: What are the advantages of data loggers?

A: In contrast to transmitting devices, data loggers retain any information on board the device, using small computer chips, and that information is later transferred to a computer—but, and this is the catch, only when the device is retrieved. The upside is that it does not take so much battery power to retain data in comparison to transmitting it, so that the devices can be smaller. They can also store data from any number of instruments that measure things about the environment through which the penguin is moving. Possible examples are: water temperature, salinity, whether the device is wet or dry (this enables researchers to know when the penguin is at the surface or out of the water), pressure (which gives depth), and speed. Geographic location is the Holy Grail for data loggers because it offers the prospect of small and cheap devices to track penguins at sea over extremely long periods. Initially there was an attempt to measure light intensity in conjunction with an accurate clock. When you think about it, this is not as daft as it sounds because, theoretically at least, wherever you are on the globe affects the amount of light you receive from the sun at any particular time of day. The problem is that, in practice, there are so many things that can temporarily affect light intensity—such as cloud cover— that the variation (what scientists like to call error) in plotting longitude and latitude this way is immense. Just recently, however, loggers have been deployed successfully that can record locations from the network of Global Positioning System (GPS) satellites. Accuracy has gone from miles to meters.

Loggers may be cheaper and smaller than those used for satellite telemetry, but they must be retrieved to get any data. If the logger falls off, if the penguin fails to return to a site where it can be recaptured, or if the penguin dies en route, all

In the Antarctic, penguins will often rest on icebergs and ice floes. It is more a means of having a breather than hitching a ride.

information is lost with it. Nevertheless, with our increased understanding of penguin behavior, improved design of loggers, and improved techniques for attaching and retrieving loggers with minimal fuss, this has become less of a problem and it is certainly the way of the future.

Q: How far do penguins travel during their migrations?

A: There has not been enough research done to be able to answer this question adequately. In most instances, the technology and techniques are still trying to catch up with the desire of the researchers to track penguins over many months. Taping devices to feathers has its limits, because drag may eventually wrench the feathers out or the devices may simply drop off. There have been some successes to date, however: Adelie Penguins tracked from Ross Island in Antarctica migrated up the western side of the Ross Sea and out to an area northwest of the Balleny Islands. In four and a half months (the longest period over which the penguins have been tracked with satellites), one bird traveled more than 1,700 miles, which means that during its entire eight-month migration its round trip might clock up more than 3,000 miles. Other Adelie Penguins on Ross Island have been found to head northeast and spend the winter among the pack-ice. Magellanic Penguins along the coasts of Argentina, and even those in the Falklands Islands, all head up to the waters off Buenos Aires that are enriched by sediments poured

from the Rio de la Plata. None of the satellite transmitters deployed on Magellanic and Rockhopper penguins tracked from the Falklands functioned for more than about three months, but in both species there were individuals that swam well over a thousand miles in two and a half months. In time, GPS loggers promise to provide us with a much better picture of penguin migration, but for now it is safe to say that offshore-feeding penguins may swim thousands of miles between breeding attempts. It is a wonder they do not get lost.

Although research is ongoing, there is still little definitive data on how far penguins migrate. Successful studies have tracked Adelie Penguins' Antarctic travels while Magellanic Penguins tracked by satellites were noted to migrate from the Falkland Islands up the coast of South America to an area enriched by the Rio de la Plata.

Navigation

Q: What are vagrants?

A: In fact, some penguins do get a bit lost. It sounds a lot like hobos hanging around the corners of the penguin world, but "vagrants" is an actual term used to describe birds that show up in the most unlikeliest of places beyond their normal or known distribution. For example, Adelie Penguins are Antarctic birds but vagrants have been picked up on many subantarctic islands and even as far north as New Zealand. Emperor Penguins, too, have occasionally made it that far north, including New Zealand, as have King Penguins, which have also been sighted in South Africa and Australia, where it is possible that they could run into a Fiordland Penguin a long way from its home. Magellanic Penguins have sometimes managed to find their way across the Pacific and end up in New Zealand and Australia, too. The thing to note about these lost souls of the penguin world is that they are largely the offshore-feeding, migratory types. It is true that a Galápagos Penguin wound up in Panama, but the suspicion has always been that it hitched a ride on a ship.

Q: How do penguins know where they are going?

A: The phenomenon of bird migration and how birds navigate has long occupied bird biologists—or ornithologists as they like to call themselves. But it is one

Below: King Penguins are creatures of the sub-antarctic, but they can turn up in such warm places as Australia and Africa.

Below right: Penguins, such as this Gentoo, must navigate without the advantages of height and some of the navigational cues that flying birds can use.

thing for a bird flying at an altitude of several hundred, if not thousands, of feet to see where it is going, quite another for a flightless bird operating at ground level across featureless ice or a featureless ocean. It has been known for some time that flying birds can make use of the sun and the stars when migrating and the same would seem to be true of penguins.

Decades ago, researchers took Adelie Penguins out onto the flat, amorphous, and white Ross Ice Shelf and let them go as if they were homing pigeons: the results showed that the penguins did not leave in a random manner but departed more or less in the same direction. At least when the sun was out. Like ancient mariners, they have learned somehow to use the sun as their compass. Yet, even when it was cloudy, although not as accurate as under sunny conditions, the penguins still managed to leave in a nonrandom manner; they still managed to head in a general direction, sort of. This redundancy is a characteristic of the migratory abilities of flying and nonflying birds: deprive them of one set of cues and they can use another.

Adelie Penguins can navigate even across the monotonous ice-covered areas of Antarctica.

Navigation on a Fine Scale

Q: How can penguins get back to their exact nest site?

A: Even if the birds use stars, sun, magnetic fields, or whatever, the extraordinary ability of penguins to end up exactly on the same nest site from one year to the next suggests that for navigation close to home, learning features of their landscape must play a role for such detailed homing. Think of it as like golf. It seems incredible that someone like Tiger Woods could use only three or four hits to get a tiny ball into a cup not much bigger than it is when he is standing more than four or five hundred yards away and cannot even see the hole. The thing is that pinpoint accuracy of the first one or two shots is not so crucial. How many times have you seen Tiger miss the fairway only to get his par? The point of those first few shots is to get to the vicinity of the hole, not in it, in the same way that the navigational abilities of

Right: Laysan Albatross on Midway Island proved that they were smarter than the military when they made their way back to the island after being taken elsewhere in an ill-advised attempt to clear them from the vicinity of the runway.

Below: Penguins, when close to shore, will often lift their heads out of the water as if to assess local landmarks.

the penguins return them to the vicinity of their colony, not the nest site. It is the last part of a golf ball's journey that requires the ultimate accuracy. Penguins can often be seen sticking their heads out of the water as they approach land, as if looking for local landmarks such as headlands or mountains or trees or who knows what. And when they are on shore, they move through the colony, stopping every now and then to look about and assess their surroundings. It seems at this finer scale, like Tiger Woods with his putter, they are using features of the landscape as small as the placement of rocks near their nests.

Q: Can penguins navigate using underwater landmarks?

A: One of the most amazing things that is emerging from the deployment of highly accurate GPS loggers on penguins

when they go to sea is that some penguins seem to be using underwater landmarks to navigate, in much the same way that pigeons can use local landmarks when flying in the air. Tracks of inshore-feeding Yellow-eyed Penguins leaving from one colony on New Zealand's southeastern coast showed that they were changing direction at a specific point on their journey, within a yard or three of each other. Investigation revealed a small underwater reef at that point. The route the penguins were taking was not just consistent between individuals, but also consistent between years. It seems possible that penguins may be able to read local underwater topography like a road map.

Q: Can penguins navigate home from an unknown starting point?

A: The most extreme navigational abilities are those that enable a bird to find its way home from an unknown starting point. It seems incredible, but the penguins' close cousins, the albatross, can do it. Albatross wander over thousands of miles of the Earth's oceans. If ever there was an excellent demonstration of their homing abilities it was during World War II: in an attempt to solve a problem of Laysan Albatross nesting on the runway at Midway Island in the Pacific, the American military came up with a solution as only they can do. They flew the albatross to various parts of the globe and released them, presumably on the basis of the military modus operandi that a problem out of sight was a problem solved. Some of the birds are said to have made it back to the airstrip before the aircraft.

Fortunately penguins tend not to nest on airstrips (although in Antarctica, the French have been known to bulldoze their nests to build a runway), but in one experiment, Adelie Penguins taken and released on one side of Antarctica eventually found their way back to their nest sites on the other side. Homing abilities are not confined to the migratory offshore-feeding penguins either. Interventions to save penguins from being oiled have sometimes seen African and Little penguins transported to distant places only for the birds to reappear at their colonies some weeks later.

Percy the Penguin was one of 20,000 African Penguins translocated to Port Elizabeth after an oil spill in 2000. Tracked using satellite telemetry, Percy swam the 500 miles back to his home on Dassen Island in just 20 days.

Migration of Juveniles

Q: Where do juvenile birds go after they fledge?

A: Like many seabirds, indeed, many animals, juvenile penguins leave home for a period of years before coming back to settle down and start families of their own. Where they go remains pretty much a mystery. It is presumed, with some justification, that they use this time to go to areas where they can get food and fatten up; areas where perhaps they do not have to compete with their older and more experienced parents. But it is really hard to tell. Data loggers using GPS to record locations are only just being refined enough to suggest that they might have the capability of tracking juveniles on migrations measured in years, not months. Of course, that is assuming that issues associated with attaching the devices to the penguins for such long periods can be solved. There is also the problem of molt. In the future, surgical implantation of devices below the skin might offer the best prospect for tracking juveniles.

Recovery of birds banded as fledglings can help draw something of a picture. Yellow-eyed Penguins from near the bottom of New Zealand's South Island have been found as far north as the East Cape on the North Island, a place where no self-respecting adult would be seen. Juvenile Little Penguins are known to disperse widely around New Zealand and Australia. Juvenile Emperor Penguins have been tracked for the first few weeks of their migration using satellite telemetry. They moved north of the Antarctic Convergence where, in contrast to the pack-ice predilections of their parents, they had to have been immersed in water all the time. There they seemed to move in an eastward direction with the prevailing current and winds: drifters as sure as any teenagers. Even though this was only the first two months of a journey that would take them years, one had already traveled nearly 1,800 miles from where it had hatched on its father's feet.

The down from the tops of their heads is the last to go as these Adelie Penguin chicks get ready to fledge. They differ from their parents by having a white chin.

Q: **How many juveniles survive the migration?**

A: Of one thing we can be certain: the juvenile migration is a dangerous venture from which many, if not most, will not return. It is estimated that less than half of the Adelie Penguin chicks that fledge on the Antarctic Peninsula survive to become breeders. For Little and Yellow-eyed penguins, the numbers seem even lower. And less than one in five Emperor chicks will survive their first year out on the high seas.

Time and time again, studies have revealed that the one really good deter-minant of whether juveniles will survive their migration is fledgling weight. How much the chicks weigh when they say good-bye to mom and dad is the best predictor of their own prospects of becoming a mom or dad. In other words, this puts the onus squarely on the parents:

if they want to be successful breeders, it is not enough just to keep their young alive until they fledge, they must fatten them up so that their chicks are the penguin equivalent of butterballs. Skinny chicks are dead chicks.

This then raises the question: Should penguin parents try to rear two chicks when food conditions are poor or would it be better to concentrate on just one?

Above: The best predictor of whether a chick will survive to breed is its mass at fledging—a fact that this Gentoo parent seems well aware of.

Left: Juvenile penguins are often shades of gray compared to the stark black-and-white world of their parents.

CHAPTER 11

PENGUINS AND PEOPLE

There is just something about penguins that humans find appealing. It is no coincidence that the highest grossing wildlife documentary of all time is *March of the Penguins.* It is no coincidence that cruises to Antarctica are promoted using pictures of penguins: people do not travel on expensive ships to the bottom of the world to see collembola—although these primitive insects are as tough any Emperor Penguin, surviving the Antarctic winter actually frozen beneath the snow. It is no coincidence that the biggest single wildlife attraction in Australia is the Penguin Parade at Phillip Island. And can it really be coincidence that Linux, the open-source computer operating software that is the darling of geeks around the world, should have a penguin as its mascot?

Yet it is a strange relationship, this one between people and penguins. We are as inclined to laugh at them as we are to admire them. We profess our love for them at the same time as we persecute them. More than half the world's remaining species of penguins are listed as endangered or vulnerable in some way. We forget that for most of their history they lived happily without us; it would be nice to think that they did not always have to live unhappily with us.

Above: A Magellanic Penguin gets a checkup at the San Francisco Zoo.

Left: A Little Penguin clad in a knitted sweater to prevent it ingesting oil after it had the misfortune to swim through an oil slick.

Cute Appeal

Q: Why do most of us like penguins?

A: This is, of course, hard to quantify and it is likely that the reasons will vary from person to person. The common denominator, however, is people's perception that penguins are in some ways like us. Ironically, it is those things that changed as a consequence of their returning to the sea and becoming more fishlike that amuse us. They walk upright like us. Their black and white attire appeals to our dress sense. They regularly trip when walking, making them the Keystone Cops of the animal world. They are Laurel to our Hardy.

So it should not have been unexpected, then, that when Kelly Tarlton's Underwater World—an aquarium in Auckland, New

Right: A penguin is the mascot for the computer operating system known as Linux.

Below: Magellanic Penguins at SeaWorld in San Diego, where penguins are kept in conditions conducive to breeding and behaving normally.

Zealand—planned to open a penguin exhibit, it would attract considerable attention. Modeled on the one at SeaWorld, San Diego, where the penguins are kept in temperature and light regimes similar to those they would experience in the wild, it was nevertheless opposed by animal rights groups that were against keeping penguins in any form of captivity.

Initially, the exhibit was forced to open using plastic penguins as stand-ins until appropriate permits could be obtained to house the real King and Gentoo penguins (which were hatched from eggs produced at SeaWorld, rather than being taken from the wild). This presented an ideal opportunity to test the effect that real as opposed to plastic penguins could have. Initial testing revealed that the majority of visitors who viewed the exhibit were unaware that penguins were birds, classifying them as fish or mammals like us. And that is it really. Logic says that if it has feathers it must be a bird, but another part of our brains says that if it walks like us, it is like us. Incidentally, people learned a lot from the exhibit regardless of whether it had plastic or real penguins in attendance, but they learned more and satisfaction levels were higher with the real thing.

Q: Why do cartoons often use penguins?

A: Over the years, penguins have proved to be great favorites of cartoonists. First, they are like little people, which helps a lot in the satirical world of black lines and one-liners. They have come to represent conformity

and uniformity. Perversely, they have also come to represent the cold, even though many penguins do not live in the cold. And, perhaps most perversely of all, they are often portrayed as inhabiting a world populated by Eskimos, igloos, and polar bears. There is a famous Gary Larson cartoon of seven penguins sharing a small ice floe with a large polar bear that is wearing a fake penguin bill tied to its muzzle as if in disguise, however poorly. One of the penguins is saying to another, "And now Edgar's gone. . . . Something's going on around here." But, it is not polar bears that penguins need to be worried about, it is people.

Although they vary in size and coloration between species, penguins are often used in cartoons as icons for conformity, uniformity, and formality. Here, a top hats and ties have been added to their black-and-white attire.

Harvesting Penguins

Q: Why did humans harvest penguins?

A: All of the terrestrial tetrapods—those land-living creatures with backbones and four legs—that have gone back to the sea have not fared well over recent times. And it is the very things that enabled

A cook skins an Emperor Penguin during Shackleton's British Imperial Trans-Antarctic Expedition of 1914–16.

warm-blooded animals to go back to the sea that have made them attractive to us: the blubber of whales and the fur of seals. What was evolution's milestone was in danger of becoming extinction's headstone. Many whales were brought to within a baleen's breath of annihilation, and many seals looked at a similar fate with their big brown eyes. Harpooned, clubbed, sliced, and boiled—it did not matter how you did it, the creatures were killed. And, as the numbers of whales and seals diminished, the whalers and sealers began to look to other quarry: penguin skins and penguin oil.

King Penguins were especially hard done by: for 100 years, the King Penguins on Macquarie Island were boiled down for their oil, completely exterminating

some colonies. On the Falkland Islands and Heard Island, they disappeared altogether. In the last few decades, with the cessation of commercial hunting, the penguins have been making a comeback. But it has been a slow business. It has been nearly a century since exploitation of King Penguins stopped on Macquarie, but it took all of 80 years for their numbers to recover.

Even if humans have not wanted penguins for their oil, their feathers or their meat—and Humboldt Penguins were plundered for all three—penguins have been killed for no better reason than to use them as bait for supposedly better-tasting food: on Gough Island in the Atlantic, fishermen baited their crayfish pots with Rockhopper Penguins.

Penguins, apparently, are an acquired taste, but desperate times call for desperate menus. Ernest Shackleton, marooned on sea-ice with little food for nearly five months, finally managed to get his men to Elephant Island where there were "a few thousand ringed [Magellanic] penguins." As hungry as he was, he was still able to remark: "The ringed penguin is by no means the best of the penguins from the point of view of the hungry traveller." Unfortunately for the starved crew of the ill-fated *Endurance*, the ringed penguins were just about to migrate. As Shackleton and his men armed themselves with "pieces of sledge-runner and other improvised clubs," the penguins took to the water and they "saw them no more." At least there was the odd nonmigratory Gentoo Penguin, which, as Shackleton observed with some satisfaction, "far surpasses the adelie in weight of legs and breast, the points that particularly appealed to us."

Q: Did humans harvest penguin eggs, too?

A: For those penguins most closely associated with human settlements—in other words, the inshore feeders of the lower latitudes—it has been their eggs rather than their bodies that have been most at risk from harvesting. During the first 90 years of the twentieth century, the number of African penguins fell by nearly 70 percent, in no small measure due to the harvesting of their eggs, which in one area alone saw more than 13 million eggs taken over a 30-year period. But it is not just the inshore-feeding penguins that suffer: eggs of Rockhopper Penguins on

Ernest Shackleton: an Antarctic explorer with a taste for adventure and the odd penguin.

Tristan da Cunha and the Falkland Islands continue to be harvested even today. And farther south, the eggs of Gentoo and Adelie penguins used to be taken by the thousands to feed the crews of ships.

King Penguins were exterminated from the Falkland and Heard islands, and much of Macquarie Island.

Habitat Destruction

Q: How does harvesting guano affect penguins?

A: Ironically, the harvesting of seabird excrement has been as lethal for African and Humboldt penguins as if they had been harvested themselves, excrement and all. On islands and coastal headlands with masses of colonial seabirds, such as pelicans and boobies, prodigious amounts of guano build up over time. But one seabird's waste is another seabird's home: penguins have learned to make their burrows in the guano deposits of the pelicans and others. The problem is that guano contains phosphates and phosphates make great fertilizer, so for centuries humans have collected the guano, often right down to bare rock, which the penguins cannot burrow in. The penguins are left with poor choices: if they nest aboveground it is too hot and they experience very poor breeding success; if they move elsewhere and burrow into sand, the burrows are prone to collapsing.

Blue-footed Boobies perch on guano-covered rocks in the Galápagos Islands. Because penguins make their nests in the guano of other seabirds, the harvesting of this waste product affects their survival.

Q: What other kinds of habitat destruction affect penguins?

A: In areas where penguins use vegetation for protection from the sun, it is the clearing of forest to make way for farming that has affected them the most. On the New Zealand mainland, Yellow-eyed Penguins used to flourish, breeding in dense forests that reached right down to sandy beaches. In the last two centuries, however, the penguins' preserve has given way to a nation of sheep. Much of the coastal forests on New Zealand's south-eastern shores have been burned and cut down to make way for grasslands. With every tree felled, the population of Yellow-eyes fell, too. A group was formed to save the penguins, but because repatriation of the forest would take more time than the penguins had, quick-growing native flaxes were planted, which provided almost instant—albeit nontraditional—Yellow-eyed Penguin breeding habitat. Although numbers of Yellow-eyed Penguins breeding on the New Zealand mainland have been slowly increasing as a consequence, the penguins are figuratively not out of the woods yet, even if literally they must feel that they are, and they remain one of the world's rarest penguin species.

In Australia it has been housing that has often affected the habitat of Little Penguins: Phillip Island lost nine of its ten breeding colonies of Little Penguins during the last century as people clambered to build holidays homes on areas used by the penguins for breeding. Little Penguins get their revenge to some extent: around Australia and New Zealand

Farming and livestock-raising has intruded on the habitat of some penguins, such as Yellow-eyed Penguins in New Zealand.

where human habitation encroaches on their habitat, Little Penguins are wont to build nests under the houses, keeping the stressed occupants awake at nights as they serenade each other with calls that are as loud as they are discordant.

For wanton destruction of penguin habitat, however, it is hard to beat the French. Between 1984 to 1992, the French government constructed an airfield to service their Antarctic base at Pointe Géologie and in the process destroyed two islands and 10 percent of the Adelie Penguin nests on the Pointe Géologie Archipelago. The population of Adelie Penguins may well have increased since then, but better food conditions and an increased availability of snow-free areas for breeding as a result of global warming are the probable causes, and not, as one publication put it, due to "the beneficence of the French."

Little Penguins sometimes lose out to humans who like the same coastal property to build their own houses on.

Introduced Predators

Q: Are penguins at risk from predators introduced by humans?

A: If becoming flightless could only have evolved in out-of-the-way places free of predators, the big risk of such a strategy was always going to be what would happen if predators eventually made it to such places. There can be no going back: penguins are as grounded as any plant. But really, it is only in the last one thousandth of one percent of their time on Earth that penguins have had to put up with humans moving into their territories and bringing with them some of the nasty creatures that prevented birds from even thinking about becoming flightless in the Northern Hemisphere.

Foxes, introduced to Australia, have become major predators of Little Penguins. Cats let loose on Dassen Island used to kill nearly one in ten African Penguin chicks. And, although the subantarctic islands may have stood as isolated bastions of penguinhood for millions of years, when the whalers and sealers arrived, they brought with them cats and rats. In addition to the damage they can inflict themselves, such animals carry ticks, fleas, and lice, which are vectors for diseases that can kill penguins and their chicks.

Controlling predators after they have been introduced to areas with penguins is a lot easier to say than to do. Five cats were taken to subantarctic Marion Island in 1948 to control mice introduced by sealers: less than 30 years later there were estimated to be more than 2,000 cats on the island, living largely off seabirds, including penguin chicks. The cats have now been eradicated from Marion Island, but in many cases it is simply too late and too unrealistic to remove introduced predators once they have become established.

Such is the case with stoats and ferrets taken to New Zealand, which have since run riot with its bird fauna, including penguin chicks. One way to dissuade such predation on the likes of Yellow-eyed Penguins might be to control not the predators but, rather, another introduced animal: the

Foxes have been introduced into Australia where they make life difficult for Little Penguins.

rabbit. Penguin chicks are easy meat for the likes of stoats and ferrets, but they are a seasonal delicacy and the stoats and ferrets need something else to eat at other times of the year. Mainly, they live off rabbits and, so, if the rabbit numbers can be kept low the numbers of predators an area can support will be reduced, lowering the risk to penguins breeding there. In Peru, there has been success in erecting predator-proof fences around mainland headlands such as Punta San Juan where Humboldt Penguins breed.

Domesticated animals that get out of control can also pose threats to penguins. Autopsies of Little Penguins found dead in northern Otago, New Zealand, showed that dogs killed one in six of them. In such instances, controlling the owners of the pets is probably the best defense.

Left: Stoats and others of their kind have been introduced to New Zealand, where they have ravaged native bird populations, including penguins.

Below: African Penguins are as tough as they are stocky, but their chicks are vulnerable to introduced predators such as cats.

Fisheries

Q: How big a problem is bycatch?

A: "Bycatch" are the living creatures that are caught unintentionally by fishing gear. Gill nets represent a hazard for penguins—a lethal hazard. More than one in ten Yellow-eyed Penguins found dead around Otago, New Zealand, was drowned in gill nets, and the evidence suggested that the numbers might actually have been twice as high. Across the Pacific, fishing around the Valparaiso region of Chile claims the lives of hundreds of penguins, mainly Humboldts. And,

Gill nets pose mortal threats to curious sea-birds, including gannets, albatrosses, boobies, pelicans—and penguins.

on the other side of South America, on the Patagonian coast of Argentina, Magellanic Penguins get caught in nets by the thousands each year, which has reduced the numbers of penguins breeding there by more than 60 percent.

The bycatch of penguins is not limited to inshore-fishing either: driftnet fishing, which uses walls of fine gill nets that drift in the open ocean, has had a significant impact on Rockhopper Penguins around the Tristan da Cunha group of islands in the South Atlantic. Evidence from fisheries in Peru suggests that penguins are more likely to be caught in drift gill nets than they are in fixed gill nets.

Large penguins, such as King Penguins, are even in danger of being killed when

Offshore feeders such as Rockhoppers are vulnerable to getting caught in the fine mesh of gill nets used in open water.

taking baited hooks, with evidence of them being caught as bycatch on Japanese longline fishing vessels in waters off Africa.

But the real problem of fisheries may not be that they kill penguins directly but that they compete with them for the same prey.

Q: Do fisheries compete with penguins for the same resources?

A: It is, with observers onboard fishing boats, a relatively simple matter to count penguins hauled up in nets or on longlines. Far more difficult to assess is the impact that fisheries may have by competing with penguins for the same prey. Overfishing of inshore-shoaling fish by purse seine fishers undoubtedly contributed to a decline in the number of African Penguins during the twentieth century, but it remains difficult to quantify the extent of the problem. Certainly, diet studies, from African to Yellow-eyed penguins, suggest that there is considerable

Left: Antarctic penguins such as Adelies and Chinstraps that rely to a large extent on krill can be adversely affected by competition with fisheries if it increases the time they take to get food for their chicks.

Below: Large penguins, such as King Penguins, are even at risk from longline fishing, where long lines of baited hooks are towed behind boats.

overlap in the fish species taken by penguins and those targeted by fisheries.

Perhaps the most potentially at risk are those high-latitude species of penguins that rely almost exclusively on krill; the likes of the Adelie and Chinstrap penguins. Although the abundance of krill is great, it also attracts a fair bit of attention from fisheries. And not because krill taste great—well they might to a penguin, but not to us. Krill are being caught by the ton largely to fatten farm animals. Offshore feeders such as Adelie Penguins operate at such a precariously poised balance that the fisheries need not take all, or even most, of the krill to affect the penguins. All they have to do is make it harder for the penguins to find krill, to delay the time they return to the nest by a day or two, and the potential for desertions by adults and starvation of chicks will be increased. Latest modeling suggests that reductions in penguin breeding success can be expected to occur as the intensity of krill fishing increases, particularly in the area around the Antarctic Peninsula.

Pollution

Q: How does oil pollution affect penguins?

A: What we take from the ocean is only half the problem; the other half is what we dump into it. And perhaps the worst offender when it comes to pollution and seabirds is oil. It is not just that oil is poisonous when ingested by penguins, it also clogs their feathers, destroying the waterproofing and insulative properties, turning their feather survival suits into mucky black cloaks of death.

It has been estimated that oil pollution may have been killing as many as 20,000 adults and 22,000 juvenile Magellanic Penguins each year along the Argentine coast. In one oil spill in Apollo Bay in Australia, more than 260 Little Penguins died as a consequence. But it was another Apollo, a ship by the name of the *Apollo* Sea, that would claim a much bigger tally: it sank in 1994 near Robben Island—the place in South Africa where Nelson Mandela had been locked up for years—releasing some 2,000 tons of oil into the sea. African Penguins died by the thousands. A rescue group, the South African National Foundation for the Conservation of Coastal Birds (SANCCOB) collected 10,000 oiled penguins and by washing them and feeding them managed to save more than they lost.

Oil-soaked African Penguins: the collateral damage in our war on the environment; these ones, the victim of an oil spill near Robben Island.

But that was not the end of it. Six years later, another ship, this one inappropriately named *Treasure*, went down in the same area with 1,300 tons of oil onboard, providing the penguins with anything but treasure. Remarkably, SANCCOB took more than 19,000 oiled African Penguins into captivity—at one time having more than 20 percent of the world's entire population of African Penguins in captivity. Remarkably, fewer than 2,000 birds died, but it would be naive to expect rescue operations could be mounted on such a scale in other places that penguins inhabit that are at risk of shipping disasters. And at any rate, although these major catastrophes capture the headlines and provide potentially large losses, they are isolated events, and it has been estimated that more penguins die due to the ever-present small oil spills that are a chronic problem with shipping. Recent efforts, however, to police the discharge of oil by ships along the Patagonian coast seems to have had a dramatic effect in terms of reducing the deaths of penguins due to oiling, so perhaps there is hope.

Oil tankers such as this often ply waters where penguins live: a potential disaster waiting to happen. It is, however, the chronic discharge of oil from ships of all types that may represent the greatest hazard.

where penguins live in association with humans. More surprising has been the discovery that even in penguins breeding in the most isolated parts of the world such as Antarctica, there are detectable levels of DDT, PCBs, and other pollutants in their blood. In other seabirds, such pollutants can cause problems such as the thinning of their eggshells, but more research must be done on penguins to know how severe the threats from pollutants are likely to be. One thing is for sure: their evolution in isolated parts of the Southern Hemisphere is no guarantee that penguins are immune to the consequences of human-induced pollution. When we pollute our environment, we pollute their environment.

Q: **What other pollutants affect penguins?**

A: Analysis of penguins for pollutants such as pesticide residues, PCBs, and mercury have, perhaps not surprisingly, shown them to be prevalent in areas

A molecule of DDT: one of the most destructive and persistent pollutants ever introduced into our ecosystems.

Global Warming

Pollution from vehicles driven on a Los Angeles freeway is affecting penguins breeding in another hemisphere.

Q: Is global warming affecting penguins?

A: Perhaps the most insidious, the most pernicious feature of the relationship between humans and penguins is that we do not even need to be near them to affect them. We can pollute half a world away and they feel the consequences. A factory in Poland, cars on a Los Angeles freeway, deforestation in Asia, all cumulatively affect the atmosphere and the climate, not just in our own backyards but in the whole world, including the world of penguins.

One consequence of the increasing temperatures of the globe over the last 60 years has been the increased frequency and intensity of El Niño events: periods when the sea surface temperatures of the southern oceans rise. Now if you like swimming, that may not sound like a bad thing, but the trouble is that a layer of warm surface water prevents upwelling of the nutrient-rich cold waters that fuel the plankton blooms on which the productivity of the seas and the penguins depend. Less productivity means less food for penguins, which means

Galápagos Penguins have been particularly hard hit by warming trends that have increased the frequency and strength of El Niño.

less food for their chicks, and that all translates into lowered breeding success. In the most extreme instances, it can mean death even for adults. More than three-quarters of the world's population of Galápagos Penguins was lost during the exceptionally strong El Niño of 1982–83, bestowing on them virtually overnight the dubious distinction of being the world's rarest penguins. The future outlook looks grim for those penguins breeding on the eastern side of the Pacific where the effects of El Niño are most keenly felt (in other words, the Galápagos and Humboldt penguins).

But it is not just the banded or *Spheniscus* penguins that are at risk: the breeding success of Little Penguins in New Zealand has been correlated with El Niño events, too. Global warming is also thought to have contributed to the decline of the Yellow-eyed Penguin. Warm periods recently have reduced the extent of sea-ice in the Terre Adelie sector of Antarctica, and the number of Emperor Penguins breeding there has

The survival of the krill favored by Antarctic penguins such as Adelies and these Chinstrap and Gentoo Penguins is dependent upon the amount of ice cover.

been halved. On the subantarctic islands there have been massive declines in the numbers of Rockhopper Penguins from the middle of the last century, with the rising sea surface temperatures and global warming implicated as the culprits.

In the Antarctic, Adelie Penguins depend, ironically, upon the cold for the over-winter survival of their main prey source: krill. Colder winters mean thicker sea-ice cover, which insulates the vulnerable young krill from the worst of the winter chill. But the frequency of cold winters with extensive sea-ice cover has been declining, and with it, the numbers of krill and the breeding success of Adelie Penguins on the Antarctic Peninsula.

Superficially at least, on the other side of the Antarctic, Adelie Penguins seemed to benefit from the climate change, with numbers of penguins breeding on Ross Island actually increasing during the 1970s and 1980s. That was until global warming struck another, monumental blow.

El Niño conditions increase sea surface temperatures in the eastern Pacific in a region coincident with the breed-ing areas of Galápagos and Humboldt penguins.

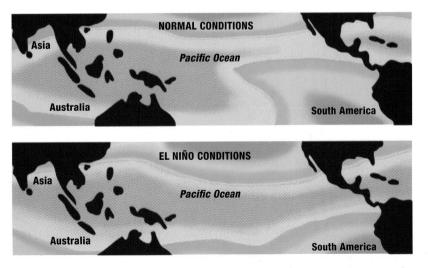

Antarctic Ice Shelves

Q: How does the break up of the Antarctic ice shelves affect penguins?

A: In March 2000, the largest iceberg (B15) ever recorded broke off the Ross Ice Shelf and became grounded near the Adelie Penguin colonies on Ross Island, along with another large berg (C16) that it dislodged when it banged into the shelf. B15 was not just a piece of ice of *Titanic*-sinking proportions, it was a small country: with an area of more than 4,200 square miles (11,000 sq km), it was somewhat larger than Jamaica. It completely altered the ice patterns around the Ross Island penguin colonies. The sea-ice did not break out, and penguins had to traipse over large tracts of ice just to get to the sea and food. For penguins breeding at Cape Royds this meant walking up to 80 miles just to dive in. It took them much longer to get to the sea and food, they used up much more energy in the process, brought back less food, and brought it back less frequently. The result: breeding success was a disaster. Zero chicks fledged from Royds that first year and fractional numbers fledged from the other colonies. And this thing was so big that it stayed, stranded, for years. Fortunately for the penguins, in 2005 the berg moved northwards, up the western coast of the Ross Sea before breaking up. If it had stayed, it could have altered the population structure and breeding of Adelie Penguins on Ross Island forever. It will certainly have affected their genetic structure.

Of the three main breeding locations for Adelie Penguins on Ross Island—capes Royds, Bird, and Crozier—it was the birds breeding at Cape Royds that were most severely affected. In the years after the initial grounding, just a smattering of chicks were fledged each year—a few hundred, when in normal times there would be a few thousand. Adelie Penguins typically exhibit what scientists call philopatry, which is just a big word that means they never leave home; they return to live and breed in their parent's place, the place of their birth. If all penguins did that then there would not be much mixing of genes between penguin colonies and we might expect genetic differences to develop over time at the reproductively isolated colonies. Analysis of their DNA shows, however, that Adelie Penguins are remarkably homogenous genetically throughout their range. Perhaps B15 can offer an explanation for this apparent paradox: faced with almost certain reproductive failure at Cape Royds, some of

A sequence of photos from a NASA satellite showing the icebergs B15 and C16 near Ross Island. The persistence of sea-ice around Ross Island is evident in the December 9, 2001, image, effectively isolating the penguin colonies there from open water.

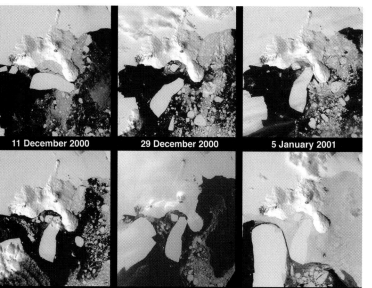

11 December 2000

29 December 2000

5 January 2001

16 January 2001

15 February 2001

9 December 2001

the breeding adults shifted to the colonies at Cape Bird and Cape Crozier. If events such as the grounding of big bergs next to penguin colonies occurred with sufficient frequency—and for evolutionary time scales that is not the same as what we might consider frequent—say, once or twice every thousand years, then it might explain why Adelie Penguins are more similar than their outwardly homebody behavior would suggest. This raises the question: Does B15 represent a regular, albeit infrequent, event or is it another indicator of global warming?

While B15 was having its calamitous impact on penguins breeding in the Ross Island area, on the eastern side of the Antarctic Peninsula, beginning January 31, 2002, a large section of the Larsen B Ice Shelf broke up. In a 35-day period, 1,250 square miles (3,250 sq km) of the ice shelf disintegrated. Ice shelves are thick plates of ice that hug the coast of Antarctica and are fed by glaciers. The Larsen B Ice Shelf is more than 700 feet thick and has been there in one form or another for the last 12,000 years. Over the last 30 years, the ice shelves around the Antarctic Peninsula have reduced dramatically in size. It is probably not too melodramatic to say that it is not just the penguins that should be scared; we should be scared too, very scared. The Ross Ice Shelf alone contains enough water to raise sea levels by more than sixteen feet worldwide. Forget bergs the size of Jamaica, if this trend continues, Jamaica will hardly exist.

The Antarctic ice shelves are thick plates of ice that are fed by glaciers.

Disease and Disturbance

Q: How prevalent is disease in penguins?

A: Relatively little is known about the prevalence of disease in penguins. Antibodies for avian malaria have been

King Penguin chicks, such as these on South Georgia Island, are naturally inquisitive, but, to minimize long-term affects on penguins, tourists should not get too close to them.

found in the blood of many penguins, and it was avian malaria that was implicated in the mysterious deaths of many Yellow-eyed Penguins more than a decade ago. A viral disease found in domestic chickens is suspected of having caused the mass deaths of hundreds of Adelie Penguin chicks. It seems that the source of such pathogens may have been chicken taken to the Antarctic to feed humans: disposed of poorly, it is thought that scavenging Skuas could have introduced the disease into the Antarctic food chain. As a consequence, several Antarctic programs now ban the use of chickens and chicken products in Antarctica.

But it is possible that we actually do not need to introduce disease, predators, or pollutants into a penguin's environment to harm it, sometimes it may be threatening enough just for us to be there.

Q: Does approaching a penguin disturb it?

A: Some species of penguins, especially those that have been exploited by humans, will panic and run if approached too closely by humans. And all penguins will panic if overflown by low-flying aircraft such as helicopters. Both helicopters and humans can elicit elevated heart rates in penguins, even if the penguins show no outward signs of stress. But the responses of penguins to humans, at least, can be quite variable depending upon the circumstances. Hearts of penguins that have been handled previously by humans start to beat rapidly when approached by humans. On the other hand, Gentoo Penguins that had not been handled, barely added an extra beat when humans approached to within 10 feet of their nests.

Q: Is tourism harmful for penguins?

A: Attempts to simulate regular visitation of penguin colonies by tourists or researchers have found that the breeding success of Adelie Penguins may be reduced relative to undisturbed colonies. This might not seem to bode well for tourism, yet it appears that penguins do have the capacity to habituate to human presence.

Measurements of the stress hormone, corticosterone, showed that Magellanic Penguins become desensitized to the presence of humans. Corticosterone is elevated in naive birds upon first seeing humans, but penguins breeding in areas frequented by tourists hardly raise an eyebrow, and certainly not a corticosteroid.

Tourism activities associated with penguins have become big business in recent years. Managed carefully, there seems good grounds for believing that controlled tourism is compatible with penguins and need not impact negatively on their breeding success. Tourists must bear in mind that sometimes being kind can also be cruel; as much as we may love them and want to approach penguins, we are best to keep our distance. Tourism does, however, hold the prospect of one indirect but huge benefit for penguins: it is impossible to look at penguins without developing an empathy for them. Every enamored tourist becomes a potential ambassador for penguins, an advocate on their behalf in the fight for their conservation.

Sometimes, even when trying to maintain a distance from them, penguins will approach humans: an Adelie Penguin walks over to a researcher and inspects his trousers.

Magellanic Penguins become habituated to the presence of humans in areas frequented by tourists.

CHAPTER 12

PENGUINS AT RISK

Penguins are resilient creatures. Tough. Knock them down and they will get up. If they fall over of their own accord, they will shake themselves and, as if nothing has happened, get on their way. Penguins will climb cliffs several hundred feet high to take food to their chicks, all the while with their belly ripped open by a leopard seal. Penguins will cope with storm and heat wave alike. They can go for weeks, even months, without food. But it would be wrong to think of penguins as invincible. The sixteen species of penguins left on Earth are but a fraction of the penguins that have cruised the southern seas since the first of them took the plunge. Half of those remaining are classified as "endangered" or "vulnerable" on the International Union for the Conservation of Nature's (IUCN) Red List—a compendium of animals at risk of extinction. Penguins have been hit by the double barrels of human attention and human neglect. We have abused them and, perhaps most unforgivably, until recently we have ignored them.

Above: Emperor Penguins obligingly pose while a photographer snaps their picture in Antarctica.

Left: Not your normal road hazard: a road sign in New Zealand warning motorists that penguins are in the area.

Penguins managed to survive as flightless birds for more than 55 million years. If they are to survive 55 more, let alone 55 million more, they will need help from us. We need to step up and make amends for what we have done.

Demographics

Q: Why are penguins so at risk?

A: Penguins are basically slow-living, slow-breeding seabirds. They have attributes that help with their resilience: they live a long time, at least relative to many other birds, and they can all fast for long periods, giving them a built-in insurance policy against periods of food shortage that might KO other birds.

Although they breed in one of the world's harshest climates, adult Emperor Penguins have the highest survival rates of all penguins.

Nonetheless, that is countered by the fact that they mature late and have low reproductive rates. They lay only one or two eggs at a time and, with the exception of a few in warmer climes, they breed only once per year.

Although annual survival rates of adults are quite high, ranging from 75 percent in Little Penguins to 95 percent in Emperor Penguins, there is a huge mortality rate of eggs, chicks, and juveniles, with the result that the vast majority of eggs do not add to the breeding population.

In other words, if their population gets severely reduced, for whatever reason, it takes them a long time to rebuild. The plankton that fuels their growth goes through a complete boom and bust cycle in a single season, but penguin populations, although they can crash almost as quickly, take years if not decades to recover even when conditions are favorable.

Q: Are inshore-feeding penguins more at risk than others?

A: Inshore-feeding penguins are the most vulnerable, it would seem. The Little Penguin and the Gentoo Penguin are the only species of inshore feeders not to have their names feature among the world's sickest populations on the IUCN's Red List. There are a number of reasons why populations of inshore-feeding penguins should be the most fragile, even if as individuals they are as tough as any offshore-feeding penguin. First, because they are the species that live in closest contact with humans, they experience the impact of our disturbance more directly. In addition, because inshore-feeding penguins have such a limited range and are nonmigratory, relying as they do on a localized and sustained food supply, they are more vulnerable to local environmental perturbations and things that affect their food supply. In contrast, the wider-ranging offshore-feeding penguins literally have more to come and go on.

Q: How can we measure the health of penguin populations?

A: Short-term studies that measure breeding success and chick survival, while useful, are not much good for telling us how well species are doing at the population level. Penguins are so long-lived, that demographic studies of penguins—which entail getting population-level data about penguins—require following known-age individuals over long periods. But that is easier said than done: How do you follow individuals in species renowned for looking alike? Enter Lance Richdale.

Above: Little Penguins, with their high survival rate, are one of the inshore feeders that have fortunately managed to avoid entering their names on the IUCN's list of sickest populations.

Left: Inshore-feeding Gentoo Penguins have also avoided entering their name on the IUCN list, but nonetheless, all penguin populations are fragile.

Lance Richdale

Q: Who was Lance Richdale?

A: As the twentieth century dawned, while penguins all over the Southern Hemisphere were scrambling to feed their chicks with little prospect that their futures were assured, in the small New Zealand town of Marton a breath of hope was drawn: on January 4, 1900, Lancelot Richdale was born. Lance Richdale was to become a knight in shining armor for the penguins, their very own Sir Lancelot. A teacher by training—his initial tertiary qualifications

Lancelot Richdale, known as the "Dr. Kinsey of the penguin world."

were in agriculture—he was an ornithologist by instinct and a scientist by dint of his actions. He studied albatross and petrels, but it was his enormously detailed long-term study of Yellow-eyed Penguins that earned him the reputation as the "Dr. Kinsey of the penguin world." For here was a man who had studied penguins closely, and his 1951 book, *Sexual Behaviour in Penguins*, became an instant classic—not least because of its methodology rather than its subject material.

Q: Was Richdale the first to band penguins?

A: In the early part of the nineteenth century, John James Audubon conducted the first-ever bird banding experiment in North America: by tying string around the legs of Eastern Phoebes, he determined that they came back to the same nests each year. It was not a lesson quickly learned. Those who studied penguins before Richdale, if they marked individual penguins at all, they did so with paint. Most notable was Murray Levick who, as member of Scott's Northern Party, spent a summer studying Adelie Penguins at Cape Adare before being forced to spend an heroic if uncomfortable winter in a snow cave. In his book *Antarctic Penguins*, published in 1914, Levick describes using red paint to follow the behavior of individual Adelie Penguins during the breeding season. Studies on Chinstrap Penguins and Gentoo Penguins followed, by amateur ornithologists, who, like Levick, used paint. The problem with paint is that it wears off, therefore providing no identification of individuals from one year to the next. Only one study had been different: as the young Lancelot Richdale was celebrating his ninth birthday, the biologist Louis Gain was applying colored celluloid rings—of the type used to mark poultry—to the legs of Gentoo Penguins on the Antarctic Peninsula. Ten months later, he recovered five, enabling him to determine that Gentoos on the peninsula, at least, go back to the same colony to breed. It was Audubon rediscovered more than it was one small step for man.

Richdale, on the other hand, made one giant leap for penguinkind. While he could not claim to be the first to band penguins, his genius was to develop and utilize banding to its full potential. He manufactured aluminum leg bands, which he used in conjunction with web punching (holes punched in the webbed feet of penguins). What distinguished Richdale's research was that he then followed individual birds continuously in a study that extended for 18 years. There was no other study with the same depth and intimacy as his.

Q: What advantages did banding penguins bring?

A: Lance Richdale's research on Yellow-eyed penguins was a landmark moment—if 18 years can be considered a moment—in the study of birds generally. He demonstrated the worth of long-term studies that followed individual animals. From his meticulously recorded data, it is possible to determine ages when penguins first attempt to breed, ages when they first breed successfully, fidelity to partners, fidelity to nest sites, lifespan, lifetime reproductive success, recruitment rates, dispersal, and so on: all important components for establishing the long-term viability of populations.

Richdale's 18-year study of Yellow-eyed Penguins was a landmark piece of research in the bird world, demonstrating the value of banding for following the lives of individuals.

> **There is probably no paper in the history of science that has involved such continuous, intimate and long-term recording of the behaviour of wild animals.**
> —Robert Cushman Murphy, Curator of birds,
> American Museum of Natural History, about Sexual Behaviours in Penguins

Banding Penguins

Q: What disadvantages did banding penguins bring?

A: Although Richdale had unequivocally demonstrated the advantages of banding penguins, the big problem with the leg bands that he developed was that they could not be seen easily when penguins were sitting on their nests. William Sladen moved them higher up, developing aluminum bands that folded around the base of the flipper. The bands had a numerical code imprinted on them and these could be read with binoculars, enabling penguins to be followed without further handling or disturbance. And that is essentially the model that has been used in penguin studies for the last 70 years. There have been variations on the theme: different metals used here, a slightly different shape used there, but they are all basically metal bands that are folded about the flipper. The great thing about flipper bands is that marked birds can be instantly recognized from a distance, whether or not the band can be read. This is especially important for population studies that rely on sightings of marked birds to establish patterns of survival and dispersal using a technique known as "mark and recapture."

There are, however, two inherent problems with banding penguins. First, there is likely to be an unknown level of band loss, which in various studies has been found to be anything from negligible up to 22 percent. It seems that both the design of bands and the expertise of those fitting them can have major influences on the level of loss. Flipper bands used in ongoing long-term studies of Magellanic and Yellow-eyed penguins—each of which uses a band that was designed specifically for the species—are applied by experienced banders and band losses are rare. Within reason, anyway, it is possible to get estimates of band loss—by double-banding birds or using them, as Richdale did, in combination with web punching—and factor that into any population estimates. It is the second problem associated with using flipper bands that is potentially much more problematic: the bands themselves may affect survival.

Flipper bands increase drag and the energy penguins consume for swimming. Another hazard is that they can constrict blood flow when the flipper expands during the process of molt. The latter is particularly a problem where bands have been incorrectly fitted by inexperienced or ignorant researchers. Although the evidence is contradictory, with some studies showing that bands negatively impact penguin survival and others showing that they do not, the hullabaloo surrounding this issue has been enough for government departments in some jurisdictions to ban banding of penguins altogether.

In captivity, plastic flipper bands that are somewhat like cable-ties can be used to mark individuals, but these are unsuitable for banding wild penguins.

This is a worrying development with regard to population studies of penguins because there is really no alternative to having some permanent, external, easily recognizable marking on individuals.

Q: Are there alternatives to banding?

A: The method that is often touted as an alternative to banding penguins is the use of implantable transponders of the type used by vets to mark dogs and horses: a coded chip is inserted under the skin of the penguin. It can be read (much like a bar-code) as long as the penguin is within a meter or so of a reader. This works well in situations where penguins can be channeled through a gate that incorporates a reader (and usually a platform to measure the weight of the bird to boot). From the point of view of population studies, however, transponders are useless because there is no external marking visible to show if a penguin, when it is sighted, is part of the study population and is wearing a transponder.

Q: Are there ways to improve flipper band design?

A: Efforts are being made to produce plastic flipper bands that are rubberized and have the capacity to expand while the animal is molting but still maintain their tension and adherence to the penguin when it is not. Although this avenue of research is potentially promising, success remains elusive and the longevity of such bands still needs to be proven. For the moment, despite their negatives, there is no real substitute for metal flipper bands. On the positive side, the studies on Magellanic and Yellow-eyed penguins have revealed that with the use of the right materials, good band design, and application by experienced banders, many of the problems of bands can be overcome.

Left: Little Penguins wearing matching leg bands.

Below: A banded Humboldt in captivity.

Counting Penguins

Q: How do we know how many penguins there are of each species?

A: Population studies have typically relied upon censusing birds to know how many there are at a given point in time. In most instances, it is clearly not possible to count all birds and various ways of estimating the population from sampling must be devised.

Yellow-eyed Penguin nests are sparsely distributed in dense vegetation, which makes locating nests and counting them a time-consuming and fraught business. Hence, to estimate the number of Yellow-eyed Penguins breeding on the New Zealand mainland, use was made of the fact that as inshore feeders they tend to make daily feeding trips when incubating their eggs, going to sea in the morning and returning in the afternoon to relieve their mates. By counting all birds departing for sea on beaches in the morning and then those arriving in the evening, it is possible with a few mathematical

Adelie Penguins return each year, literally by the thousands, to breed in colonies around the Antarctic.

shenanigans to convert such beach traffic into a reasonably reliable estimate of the number of breeding pairs.

Adelie Penguins have typically been censused much more directly. For decades now, every single nest at the Northern Rookery at Cape Bird, Ross Island, has been counted. Initially this was done by sending in a team of three census takers armed with maps and mechanical counters. They would independently count each subcolony and, as long as their results agreed, they would continue onto the next. If they did not, they would recount that subcolony until their results were within 5 percent of one another. It was labor-intensive and, even in the long days afforded by the Antarctic summer, it would take five days to count about 60,000 nests. At a certain point, someone figured that there must be a better way and so they compared results obtained from the ground count with those obtained by photographing the colonies from the air. This has proved effective

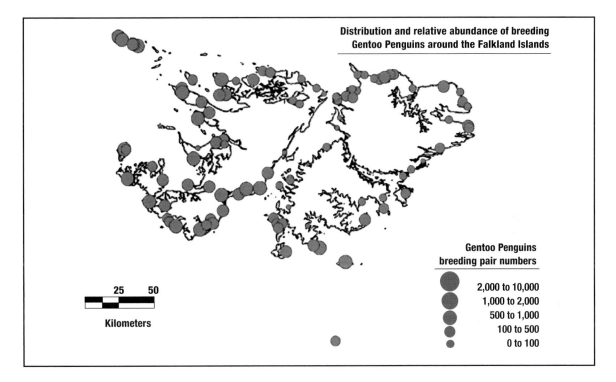

Distribution and relative abundance of breeding Gentoo Penguins around the Falkland Islands

25   50

Kilometers

Gentoo Penguins breeding pair numbers

2,000 to 10,000
1,000 to 2,000
500 to 1,000
100 to 500
0 to 100

and easier to do, and now all penguin colonies in the Ross Sea area are routinely overflown and photographed to provide a visual and numerical record of their numbers. It is important when making comparisons from one year to the next that the penguins get counted at the same part of the breeding cycle. For the Adelie Penguins, the best time to photograph the colonies is just after egg-laying: the females have departed and left the males on the eggs alone and, by then, those unable to get a mate have largely left too; and yet, at that early stage, egg losses are minimal and most nests are still intact. Hence, the number of penguins photographed in a subcolony gives a pretty good approximation of the number of breeding pairs.

For counting most colonies of penguins, however, a subsample is counted and the numbers extrapolated from there based upon the area covered by the nesting birds. Although less accurate, this is not as hit-and-miss as it might sound because, like many colonial seabirds, most penguins tend to nest at regularly spaced distances from their neighbors, in other words, at a constant density. In the case of Antarctic penguins, it is even possible to use satellite photographs of penguin colonies and then estimate numbers based upon the area covered by guano, given the regularly spaced intervals of penguin nests (about two-and-a-half feet), which are often described as being "pecking distance" apart.

The distribution and abundance of Gentoo Penguins breeding around the Falkland Islands.

Penguins as Bioindicators

Q: Can penguins do anything to help us conserve them?

Right: The Southern Ocean has had fewer surface ship surveys than any other ocean basin, so that there is very little detailed information: it is but one opportunity to use penguins to gather data about the oceans.

Below: Monitoring the breeding and behavior of Antarctic penguins such as Emperors and Gentoos can tell us as much about the health of the Antarctic ecosystem as it can about the penguins.

A: In some ways, perhaps penguins should not be seen as victims in our push to stuff up the planet but as allies in our fight to save it. The quasigovernmental organization, the Committee for the Conservation of Antarctic Marine Living Resources—known by the somewhat smaller mouthful, CCAMLR—has been charged with the task of not just protecting penguins in the southern seas, but the entire marine ecosystems of the Antarctic and subantarctic. On one hand, they

function to put protective measures in place that conserve the likes of the penguins. On the other, the scientists involved in CCAMLR have recognized the value of drafting penguins into the fight to save them. Penguins travel far and wide to get resources from the marine environment, and then return to a known base. Why not, someone suggested, harness the penguins as information gatherers to monitor the health of the Antarctic marine ecosystem? With that in mind, CCAMLR collates the monitoring of penguin colonies and specific parameters associated with their breeding: a key one is the duration of their feeding trips at sea. If penguins find it harder to get food, for whatever reason, they will take longer to return. In essence, this provides a simple snapshot of the health of the marine ecosystem. Although increased foraging trip times could potentially seriously impact the penguins themselves—increasing desertion and starvation rates—in the first instance, they can be viewed as a diagnostic indicator that there may be something wrong. Penguins can be for the seas what canaries are to mineshafts.

Q: **Why not use penguins to map the oceans?**

A: Recent work on penguins has high-lighted the possibility of going one step further and encouraging a vocational shift for the penguins, from doctor to surveyor. The aim here is to utilize pen-guins as mappers of our ocean space, as animoid robots if you will. By deploying penguins with loggers that measure such features of the environment as salinity, temperature, and depth, in association with highly accurate GPS locations, it is possible to build up a three-dimensional map of the underwater world. Sonar and the like can let us map the seafloor, but penguins can help us map the water column above it. The penguin-gathered information takes on extra value when it is combined with satellite imagery, which can measure what is happening at the sea surface, such as chlorophyll concentrations, sea-surface temperatures, and the degree of ice cover. With the help of the penguins, it becomes potentially possible not just to identify areas of high and low productivity, but also to monitor changes in those areas and understand the processes that affect them.

As camera gear gets smaller, there have even been attempts to fit cameras to penguins, so that scientists can see what the penguin sees. Penguins would be no good at all as camera operators for a feature film as they are notori-ously hard to direct—do not hold your breath waiting for *March of the Humans*—but they are much cheaper to use than submarines and can provide us with a unique window into the underwater world.

Sometimes we use windows of another kind, real glass windows, to look in on the world of penguins.

Unlike Narcissus discovering his image in a pool, a Snares Penguin is more interested in what is under the water than what is in the reflection.

Penguins in Captivity

Q: Is it good to have penguins in captivity?

A: Penguins are such fascinating creatures for us, yet most of us do not live near penguins. As a consequence, there has been a huge demand to take penguins into captivity and put them on display, with the result that there are literally thousands of penguins in captivity

Part of the problem was that mortality rates of penguins in zoos were often high, meaning that there was a never-ending market for the exporters. Techniques for looking after penguins in captivity, however, have improved markedly: disease can be managed, there is better nutrition and understanding of their dietary needs, and, perhaps most important, better understanding of their behavioral requirements. As a consequence, many zoos and other places where penguins are kept in captivity now have very successful breeding programs and are able to contribute to the conservation of penguins, as well as help to educate the public about penguins and the difficulties they face. The upshot of these captive-breeding programs is that the live export of penguins from the wild has, mercifully, become nearly nonexistent.

Q: Are penguins at SeaWorld happier?

A: The SeaWorld parks and aquaria in the United States have in captivity more than half the world's species of penguins:

Right: A Depression-era sign for a penguin exhibit at the Philadelphia Zoo: we are attracted to penguins in the good times and the bad.

Below right: A captive Humboldt Penguin under artificial lights that are regulated to imitate lighting conditions in the wild.

VISIT THE ZOO

worldwide in zoos and aquaria. This was not necessarily good for the penguins, which were (and unfortunately still often are) confined to a concrete enclosure with a puddle for a pool. More than 3,500 Humboldt Penguins were exported to zoos from Peru in the 1970s, causing the wild population to decline. Rockhopper Penguins on Gough Island did not fare much better.

Emperor, King, Adelie, Gentoo, Chinstrap, Rockhopper, Macaroni, Magellanic, and Humboldt penguins. The thing that distinguishes these parks is that they keep the animals under conditions that simulate those in the wild in terms of temperature, light regimes, and ice. No concrete pads for these zoos. All nine species breed in captivity, and SeaWorld forms part of the American Zoo and Aquarium Association's species survival plan for penguins, which coordinates species-level management of penguins in captivity with, among other things, the aim of maintaining genetically diverse self-sustaining populations. But it has not been a road without difficulty or criticism. Today the vast majority of penguins on display in North American zoos were hatched in captivity, but before SeaWorld managed to get its breeding program anywhere near self-sustaining, they took thousands of penguin eggs from the wild. Most tragically, in December 1975, a fire killed 60 Emperor Penguins, which were being held in quarantine after having been captured from the Ross Island area of Antarctica. The Emperor Penguin colony at Cape Crozier, Ross Island, is the only breeding place for Emperor Penguins in the vicinity and at the time comprised about 300 birds.

For those 60 Emperor Penguins, huddled together while an electrical malfunction in a refrigeration system turned cold into hot, ice into fire, being taken from Cape Crozier was dreadful. But just getting to Crozier could be a wretched experience for some.

Above: King Penguins are provided with a snowy home at SeaWorld.

Below: Magellanic Penguins calling and engaging in normal pairing behavior in a zoo.

The Greatest Penguin Story Ever Told

Q: Why would anyone trek to Cape Crozier in winter?

A: It may well qualify as the greatest story ever told. Certainly, it is often cited as the greatest Antarctic story of all time. That story is Aspley Cherry-Garrard's book *The Worst Journey in the World*. In it, he describes how he, Edward Wilson, and Birdie Bowers (two men who would subsequently perish beside Scott on the return march from the South Pole) traveled from Scott's base camp at Cape Evans on Ross Island to the Emperor Penguin colony at Cape Crozier on the other side of the island. Under normal circumstances this would be no mean feat because the intervening land is covered in snow and ice, with crevasses nearly as deep as the mountains are high. The thing was that Wilson, the surgeon accompanying Scott's expedition who otherwise moonlighted as the expedition's biologist and artist, wanted to collect an Emperor Penguin egg because he thought the penguins were primitive and might somehow provide the missing link between reptiles and birds. He wanted to collect Emperor Penguin embryos in the hope they would show something of this transition from the scaled to the feathered. As far as anybody could tell, the Emperor Penguin bred during the winter, which meant making the trek in the darkness and mind-numbing cold that is the Antarctic winter.

The thing that distinguishes Cherry-Garrard's account from those of other Antarctic pioneers is not just the unbelievable hardships and deprivations of an

Above: A painting of midnight in Antarctica by Edward Wilson: surgeon, biologist, artist, survivor of *The Worst Journey in the World*, and, ultimately, dead companion for Scott.

Right: "The Emperors Rookery," a sketch by Wilson of the Emperor Penguin colony at Cape Crozier.

undertaking that bordered on madness, but the peerless quality of the writing. It opens famously with:

> *Polar exploration is at once the cleanest and most isolated way of having a bad time which has been devised. . . . It is more lonely than London, more secluded than any monastery, and the post comes but once a year.*

The men pulled sleds through the eternal night in wind and temperatures that froze their clothes instantly (there were no modern fabrics or insulation: they wore the same woolen underwear that your grandmother might have worn); where the harnesses of the sled were rendered as rigid ice sculptures that could take them hours to strap into; where their breath and perspiration turned against them and became sheets of ice against their bodies. In mid-July, they established a camp at the base of Mount Terror and over the next several days managed to work their way painstakingly across the ridges of sea-ice to the Emperor Penguin colony, from which they collected five eggs. Two were broken in the struggle to return to the camp, and then a blizzard struck, blowing the canvas roof off their shelter. For two days they lay huddled in their reindeer sleeping bags in the darkness, as exposed to the worst of the Antarctic winter as any Emperor Penguin, covered in snow, without food or water save for the ice they sucked from the insides of their sleeping bags, as the blizzard raged about them and death seemed but one hypothermic moment away. To

cut a great story short, eventually they would make it back to the relative warmth and comfort of the hut at Cape Evans.

And, at the risk of spoiling the story by revealing its ending, Cherry-Garrard would deliver the Emperor Penguin embryos to the British Museum of Natural History, where it took 21 years before someone examined them and pronounced the embryos as having absolutely no bearing on the relationship between reptiles and birds.

Fortunately, for the rest of us, there are easier ways to see penguins in the wild.

Top: "Emperors Barrier and Sea Ice," another of Edward Wilson's Antarctic sketches.

Bottom: Lieutenant Henry Robertson Bowers, Dr. Edward A. Wilson, and Aspley Cherry-Garrard on the journey to Cape Crozier.

Seeing Penguins in the Wild

Q: **Where are the best places to see penguins in the wild?**

A: There is a veritable tourist industry based around cruises to the Antarctic and the subantarctic islands with the headline act the opportunity to see penguins. These are, by necessity, expensive and the places available limited. They are likely to appeal most to the wealthy or the extremely dedicated penguinophile. For most people, then, it is not possible to get ready access to Emperor, Adelie, Chinstrap, Gentoo, King, Macaroni, Rockhopper, Erect-crested, or Snares penguins. Even for those who can afford cruises, the likes of the Snares and Antipodes Islands are so heavily protected that visitors are not allowed to land and the Snares and Erect-crested penguins must be glimpsed from the water. The Galápagos is not too much different: as out of the way as the Snares and Antipodes, as expensive, and the access by tourists is controlled just as surely. For anyone who can afford a cruise around the Galápagos, the Antarctic Peninsula, or the subantarctic islands, these are wonderful experiences where penguins can still be seen in their natural near-pristine environments.

There are a lot of places, however, where penguins are much more accessible. One of these is Punta Tombo in Argentina, where buses truck in thousands of tourists to a colony where it is possible to walk, within controlled areas, among the half million Magellanic Penguins that breed in burrows there. In South Africa there are many places to see African Penguins: at Boulders Beach or

Tourist ships allow people with sea legs and deep pockets to experience Antarctic penguins such as these Gentoos.

Mossel Bay, penguins share the sand with the locals. For drama, Robben Island is hard to beat: a tourist attraction mainly because of the prison where Nelson Mandela was incarcerated, penguins can be seen breeding with the Cape Town skyline and Table Mountain providing an impressive backdrop.

Humboldt Penguins are viewable at numerous locations along the coast of Peru and Northern Chile. The mainland colony at Punta San Juan, Peru, and the near-coastal Pan de Azucar Island, Chile, are perhaps the most accessible for tourists. At Otway Bay at the bottom of Chile, there is a well-established ecotourism venture featuring Magellanic Penguins breeding before the equally photogenic peaks of Torres del Paine. If you are able to get an aircraft to the Falklands, there you may see King, Magellanic, Rockhopper, and Gentoo penguins. Sea Lion Island is an especially good vantage point—although once again this is an expensive option.

Probably the most famous, most successful, and most accessible tourist operation involving penguins is that of Penguin Parade at Phillip Island, just south of Melbourne in Australia. It is second only to the Great Barrier Reef as Australia's premier tourist attraction. On any given night there are likely to be more than 3,000 visitors and as many as 10,000 sitting in the stands by the seashore to watch the arrival of hundreds of Little Penguins.

A similar operation was started on a smaller scale at Oamaru in New Zealand. In many respects, New Zealand is as much

Humboldt Penguins are readily accessible to tourists at numerous coastal locations in Peru and Chile.

the capital for penguin visitors as it is for penguins. Access to Little Penguins can be found around virtually the entire coastline. At sites such as Pilot's Beach on the Otago Peninsula, it is possible to hang out and watch the Little Penguins come ashore for no charge. The same is true of Yellow-eyed Penguins, with the Department of Conservation maintaining free viewing hides at Sandfly Bay and in the Catlins. Across the other side of New Zealand's South Island, Fiordland Penguins may similarly be viewed wild and free (in every sense of the word) in Fiordland National Park.

To see penguins in the wild, it is a given that you must be in the Southern Hemisphere, but beyond that there are plenty of options, from the inexpensive to the expensive. Penguins have proved remarkably resilient to carefully managed ecotourism and, more than that, ecotourism has been good for penguins: it creates penguin ambassadors, people who will look out for them.

Penguins and the Future

Q: What does the future hold for penguins?

A: Overall the future does not look too bright for penguins. The situation is most grim and most immediate for some of the inshore feeders found at lower latitudes. Galápagos Penguins seem to be in particular trouble. There are probably fewer than 1,500 pairs left and those that remain have few options available to them: they either get their food around the Galápagos or they do not get it at all. With the frequency and intensity of El Niño apparently on the rise, their already battered and small population does not have much to come on, just enough to

go on. You can run mathematical models and population viability analyses until the cows come home, but they cannot alter those essential facts. Even then, the models agree on one thing: the long-term viability of the Galápagos Penguin population is bleak. Sadly, the Galápagos Penguin's best bet for immortality may be in captivity, although it is one of the few species of penguins not to be found in captivity, and the wild population cannot spare the numbers.

New Zealand's Yellow-eyed Penguin and Fiordland Penguin are not much better off with total populations around 2,000 to 3,000 pairs. In their favor, the stronghold for the Yellow-eyed Penguin remains the relatively isolated and protected subantarctic Campbell Island and the Auckland Islands. Similarly, the Fiordland Penguin has the good fortune to inhabit an area that is largely within the protected confines of a World Heritage Site. It is their narrow breeding distribution rather than absolute numbers that may be more of a liability for Fiordland Penguins, making them susceptible to changes that occur on a local scale. It is a vulnerability they share with Galápagos, Snares, and Erect-crested penguins.

Protecting the places where penguins breed, though, is only half the story— and possibly not even half the problem. Penguins spend most of their lives at sea and it is the sea that sustains them. With global warming wafting over the southern strongholds where up until now they have been able to persist in splendid isolation, even those species not currently defined as threatened

Galápagos Penguins have little to look forward to: their future appears none too bright.

are looking increasingly vulnerable. Chinstraps, Adelies, Kings, Rockhoppers, and Macaronis—all offshore feeders—number in the millions of pairs, but as the massive declines in Rockhopper numbers throughout most of their range in recent years has demonstrated, even the populous can become the depauperate if conditions at sea change. The weak do not get to inherit the Earth, just vanish from it.

In an evolutionary sense, becoming flightless made penguins strong, enabling them to dive deep and allowing them to outcompete other animals for resources that the sea had on offer. But it was an evolutionary strategy predicated on there being no significant predators; it was a plan hatched in a world without humans. We have changed all that. We have turned advantage into disadvantage for the penguins. We have made flightlessness not an asset but a liability. Ironically, if they are to have a hope, if they are to have a future, they must depend on us.

Q: **What can we do to help penguins?**

A: There are a number of things we can do, must do. First, we must put pressure on governments and the appropriate authorities to protect the remaining breeding areas of penguins. We should work to establish marine reserves where appropriate, and protect penguins from competition with fisheries, including practices to mitigate bycatch. We must reduce pollution, especially oil pollution from shipping; we should support research on penguins and programs designed to monitor penguins; and we can join groups that restore habitat for penguins. All those things we can do directly for the penguins. But the truth is that the precarious position of penguins is largely not a consequence of threats that are peculiar to them, but a consequence of the way we treat the planet. Saving penguins is not really about saving penguins; it is about saving every living thing—all of us.

The next step for penguins is in our hands: we must act now to ensure that this Yellow-eyed Penguin, and others of its kind, have better prospects ahead of them.

Studying Penguins

Lloyd Spencer Davis inside Captain Robert Falcon Scott's hut at Cape Evans, Ross Island. It was from here that Scott set out on his march to the South Pole: his bed still awaits his return.

Q: Why should someone study penguins?

A: To help penguins survive, we need to understand them, their biology and their needs. We can only gain that understanding from research.

Q: What is it like to study penguins in Antarctica?

A: Studying penguins in Antarctica has its own special magic, its own special appeal. There is nothing that can compare with the excitement of being dropped off by helicopter at a place like Cape Bird, Ross Island, for a three-and-a-half month stay with the enormity of the task before you matched only by the scale of the seemingly endless and empty environment into which you have stepped. Except that it is not as empty as your think. You quickly discover a few penguins in an area that will soon be home to more than 60,000.

Cape Bird is an impossibly beautiful place: hard to imagine, dangerous, lethal, and yet seductive at the same time. A large glacier, the Mount Bird ice cap, is wrapped around the colony, cradling bird and man equally in its crevassed arms; or perhaps that should be imprisoning, because there is a little beach to the south but otherwise nowhere else to go. Large icebergs and pack ice float by on blue seas, changing the vista from one spectacular minute to another. Killer whales break the surface with the cracking sound of guns, and seals—that equally deserve the name killer if the whales had not beaten them to it—patrol the icy margin where the land meets the sea. Beyond, there is not a horizon, but a painting: the Royal Society Mountain Range is not a backdrop as much as it is a work of art, a place that draws the eyes. And yet, for all the stark beauty apparent on that first cold day, it will be a lonely knee-high black-and-white penguin waddling up the snow-covered beach that will steal your heart.

From that moment, penguins are bound in many ways to become your life as you live in polar tents that Scott himself might have used and study penguins throughout the nightless days. You will want to go back, season after season. You will have joined the tiny band—a few hundred souls, no more—who study penguins and provide the answers upon which the penguins' futures depend.

Q: Is research on penguins valuable from other places?

A: You can have a memorable time studying penguins anywhere and your results will be just as valuable as those from locations such as the Antarctic, perhaps more so, because it is the penguins breeding in the lower latitudes in closest association with humans that are most at threat. You will remember crawling across seaweed at night as you squeeze through a cave in search of Little Penguins as much as you will remember your first day with Adelies. You can conduct research on Galápagos Penguins in the Galápagos, Fiordland Penguins in Fiordland, Snares Penguins in the Snares, and Erect-crested Penguins in, well, the Antipodes. And in these, and every other

place and time you will be with penguins, neither you nor the penguins should have reason to regret it. Their survival is literally in your hands: you are their doctor and science is their medicine.

Someone once said, when asked if they wanted to know the identity of the bird they were looking at, "No, it is enough to know that it is a beautiful bird." And really, whatever you may or may not take from a book such as this, the one thing upon which we should all agree is that it is enough that penguins are beautiful birds.

Long may they live.

Emperor Penguins in front, the Royal Society Mountain range behind: views do not come better than this.

Glossary

ALCIDAE. A family of small to medium-sized marine diving birds. Some, such as auks, bear a superficial resemblance to penguins, but they are not related.

ANTARCTICA. The southernmost continent, which includes the South Pole, and is 98 percent covered in ice.

APTENODYTES. The genus that includes the King and Emperor penguins.

BANDED PENGUINS. Name given to the four species of penguins belonging to the genus *Spheniscus* because they appear to have black bands on their plumage. Sometimes called the ringed penguins for the same reason.

BROOD CHICKS. Chicks that hatch from a single clutch of eggs. Brood size is, therefore, the number of chicks that parents must rear, which can be one or two for penguins.

BROOD PATCH. An area without feathers on the abdomen of birds that is infused with blood vessels and is used to keep eggs warm when they are being incubated.

BROOD REDUCTION. The process by which the size of the brood is reduced. In some instances this can be facultative, in that it occurs only if conditions do not allow the parents to rear all the chicks in their brood. In crested penguins it is obligate; the parents lay two eggs but only ever rear one chick, irrespective of conditions.

BYCATCH. Species caught unintentionally in fishing nets or on fishing lines.

COLONY. A group of birds breeding within a well-defined area. In the past, within the penguin literature, the term *colony* was often used to describe the discrete breeding groups that should most properly be called subcolonies. The overall collection of subcolonies within a distinct area (which was often termed a *rookery*) is most analogous to the colonies of other seabirds and so penguin biologists now refer to that as a colony.

CLUTCH. Eggs laid by a female in a single breeding attempt. Clutch size is, therefore, the number of eggs laid by the female. For penguins, this is typically one or two.

CONVERGENT EVOLUTION. The process by which unrelated groups of animals or plants exhibiting similar lifestyles in similar environments can come to resemble each other superficially because natural selection promotes similar adaptations.

COURTSHIP PERIOD. The period from when male and female penguins arrive at their colony for breeding, up until the time their eggs are laid. During this time, pair formation and copulation occurs.

CRÈCHE. A group of chicks from different nests that forms when their parents leave them unattended. In addition to penguins, flamingos and eider ducks, for example, form crèches.

CRESTED PENGUINS. Name given to the five species of penguins belonging to the genus *Eudyptes* because they have yellow or orange crests above their eyes.

DOWN. Very fine feathers that cover chicks and provide excellent insulation.

ECSTATIC DISPLAY. Behavioral display given by male penguins; used to attract females.

EUDYPTES. The genus that includes the crested penguins: Snares, Fiordland, Erect-crested, Macaroni, and Rockhopper penguins.

EUDYPTULA. The genus that includes the Little Pengiuin.

FEATHERS. Filamentous outgrowths of the skin that are characteristic of birds. They form the outer layer, helping to provide insulation.

FLEDGING. The moment when chicks become independent of their parents and fend for themselves.

GALÁPAGOS ISLANDS. A group of islands lying on the Equator in the Pacific Ocean about 600 miles west of Ecuador, to which they belong. They were the site for some of Charles Darwin's most important discoveries about evolution.

GLOBAL WARMING. A process of climate change that has seen average temperatures on Earth increase markedly from the middle of the twentieth century onward.

GONDWANA. A supercontinent that included most of the Southern Hemisphere landmasses (including Antarctica, Africa, South America, Australia, and New Zealand—in other words, all the places where penguins live or have lived) before continental drift split them apart about 167 million years ago.

GUARD STAGE. The early days of a penguin's life when one of its parents must remain with it at all times while the other goes off to sea in search of food.

HATCHING INTERVAL. The time between the hatching of the first chick from a single clutch and the second; usually only a day or two.

INCUBATION PERIOD. This is the period from laying until the hatching. In all penguins, it is more than a month.

INSHORE FEEDERS. Penguins that typically feed close to shore (less than 12 miles), usually remaining resident at their breeding grounds throughout the year and mostly breeding at lower latitudes.

KRILL. Small shrimplike crustaceans that form part of the zooplankton. They swarm in great densities in the waters of the Southern Ocean and are a primary source of food for many penguins.

LATITUDE. The angular measurement in degrees (from 0 degrees at the Equator to 90 degrees at the North or South Pole) that a place on the Earth is north or south of the Equator. Low latitudes, therefore, are those locations close to the Equator, while high latitudes are those close to the poles.

LEOPARD SEAL. A seal belonging to the family Phocidae. Going by the scientific name *Hydrurga leptonyx*, they live in waters around Antarctica and range as far north as the subantarctic islands. Ferocious predators of penguins, they characteristically skin their prey by swinging it from side to side.

MATE CHOICE. The process by which organisms chose partners for sex. It tends to lead to selection for characteristics that make an animal attractive to the opposite sex. It is one component of sexual selection; the other being competition between members of the same sex for access to members of the opposite sex.

MEGADYPTES. The genus that includes the Yellow-eyed Penguin.

MELANIN. A group of chemicals that act as a pigment in animals, typically producing dark colors such as black.

MIGRATION. The seasonal movement of animals between the location in which they breed and the location where they spend the off-season. Young penguins may undergo extended migrations before returning to their colonies to breed.

MOLT. The process by which a bird replaces its feathers with new ones.

MONOGAMOUS. Having only one mate during a breeding season or during the breeding life of a pair.

MUTUAL DISPLAY. Behavioral display between a pair of penguins; used for identity and to reinforce the pair-bond.

OFFSHORE FEEDERS. Penguins that typically feed a long way from their colonies (usually ten miles or more), particularly during the incubation period. They tend to be migratory penguins that breed mostly at higher latitudes.

PHILOPATRY. Returning to breed in the same place. Penguins generally exhibit natal philopatry, eventually breeding in the vicinity of where they were hatched.

PORPOISING. Leaping clear of the water when surfacing to breathe, while at the same time moving forward at speed. The smaller penguins use this form of locomotion when moving quickly through water.

PYGOSCELIS. The genus that includes, Adelie, Gentoo, and Chinstrap penguins.

SEX RATIO. The ratio of males to females in a population.

SEXUAL DIMORPHISM. The differences between males and females. In penguins, despite being largely monomorphic (that is, males and females look the same), there are slight differences between the sexes in size, with males typically being larger than females.

Skua. Gull-like seabird belonging to the family Stercorariidae. One of the major predators of penguin eggs and chicks.

Southern Hemisphere. The half of the Earth south of the equator.

sperm competition. An aspect of sexual selection that occurs after insemination to enhance the prospects a male's sperm will fertilize a female's eggs.

Spheniscidae. The biological family to which all penguins belong.

Spheniscus. The genus that includes the ringed or banded penguins: Galápagaos, Humboldt, Magellanic, and African.

subantarctic. The regions just north of the Antarctic Circle.

telemetry. Technology that allows remote measurements to be made. For studies of penguins, this has often involved monitoring their locations using radio signals (radiotelemetry) or satellites (satellite telemetry).

temperate. Temperate latitudes are those that lie between the tropics and the polar circles. In the Southern Hemisphere the temperate zone extends from the Tropic of Capricorn (23° 26′ 22″ S) to the Antarctic Circle (66° 33′ 39″ S).

thermoregulation. Maintaining a body temperature within certain limits irrespective of the ambient temperature.

toboggan. A form of locomotion in which the penguin lies on its belly and pushes itself along the ice with its flippers and feet.

upwelling. The process whereby cold nutrient-rich bottom waters are brought up to the surface. In combination with the warmer temperatures and light, the nutrients fuel the plankton blooms that lead to high productivity in areas of upwelling.

vertebrates. The group of animals with backbones or spinal columns. They are put together in a subphylum called Vertebrata.

warm-blooded. Animals that maintain a constant body temperature irrespective of the ambient temperature. Referred to as homeotherms.

An Adelie Penguin.

Further Reading

Books

Ainley, David G. *The Adélie Penguin: Bellweather of Climate Change*. New York: Columbia University Press, 2002.
A recent book that details the behavior of Adelie penguins in response to changing climatic variables.

Ainley, David G., Robert E. LeResche, and William J. L. Sladen. *Breeding Biology of the Adelie Penguin*. Los Angeles: University of California Press, 1983.
A compendium of detailed information from a long-term study of known-age birds.

Dann, Peter, Ian Norman, and Pauline Reilly, eds. *The Penguins: Ecology and Management*. Chipping Norton, New South Wales, Australia: Surrey Beatty & Sons, 1995.
A collection of invited papers from the Second International Conference on Penguins.

Davis, Lloyd Spencer. *Penguin: A Season in the Life of the Adélie Penguin*. San Diego: Harcourt Brace, 1994.
Antarctica as seen through the eyes of a penguin.

———. *The Plight of the Penguin*. Dunedin, New Zealand: Longacre Press, 2001.
Winner of the New Zealand Children's Book of the Year Award, 2002.

Davis, Lloyd S., and John T. Darby, eds. *Penguin Biology*. San Diego: Academic Press, 1990.
A text that brings together the work of the world's major penguin researchers.

Davis, Lloyd Spencer, and Martin Renner. *Penguins*. New Haven: Yale University Press, 2004.
An academic account of penguins, especially with respect to how feeding distance affects virtually every aspect of their lives.

Levick, G. Murray. *Antarctic Penguins*. London, England: Heinmann, 1914.
The first really comprehensive book on penguins.

Emperor Penguin chick.

Richdale, Lancelot Eric. *Sexual Behavior in Penguins*. Lawrence: University
      of Kansas Press, 1951.
A landmark book on penguins that demonstrated the value of following marked individuals.

———. *A Population Study of Penguins*. Oxford, England: Oxford University Press, 1957.
A classic study that set the standards for bird research for many years to come.

Stonehouse, Bernard, ed. *The Biology of Penguins*. Baltimore: University Park Press, 1975.
A collection of scientific papers on penguins that was the first really serious penguin book in a post-Richdale era.

Williams, Tony D. *The Penguins*. Oxford, England: Oxford University Press, 1995.
A great reference on penguins that gathers together data for all species.

Films

The World of Penguins. Available from WNET Video Distribution, South Burlington, Vermont.
A multi-award-winning documentary that covers all penguins.

March of the Penguins. Warner Independent Pictures.
Academy award–winning documentary about Emperor Penguins.

Web Sites

Antarctic Connection
www.antarcticconnection.com/antarctic/wildlife/penguins/
index.shtml
General information and quick facts about penguins, species by species.

PenguinScience.com
www.penguinscience.com
A research program studying the population biology of Adelie Penguins.

PenguinWorld
www.penguinworld.com
Reference source for all things penguin.

Te Ara: The Encyclopaedia of New Zealand
www.teara.govt.nz/EarthSeaAndSky/BirdsOfSeaAndShore/Penguins/en
A succinct encyclopaedia entry on penguins.

New Zealand Penguins
www.penguin.net.nz
An extensive site covering penguin species found in the New Zealand region.

At the Smithsonian

Although no live penguins inhabit the National Zoo, the Smithsonian Institution offers plenty of opportunities for the public to learn about these fascinating birds. Most of the Smithsonian's penguin research is done by the National Museum of Natural History's Department of Vertebrate Zoology and is maintained and housed by what is still known in ornithological circles as the United States National Museum. The research includes photographs, eggs, and even preserved specimens of more than 9,600 species of birds, including many kinds of penguins, making it the third-largest bird collection in the world. Although not open to the public, the Smithsonian's Bird Division serves as a research hub for many ornithologists, and also loans out up to 2,000 specimens a year to other institutions, including other Smithsonian branches.

One exhibit that gave the public access to research about penguins and other birds was The Bird Hall, which recently ended its run at the National Museum of Natural History. The exhibit offered dioramas of birds from 27 orders, including extinct species. Both Emperor and Adelie penguins were featured in this gallery, depicted in their natural Antarctic environment. Although this exhibit is now closed, interested parties can still see experience The Bird Hall online by visiting www.mnh.si.edu/museum/VirtualTour/Tour/First/Bird/bird3.html. NMNH has also backed researched expeditions to the Galápagos Islands, home to the penguin species named after them.

The Smithsonian's National Museum of Natural History on the Mall in Washington, D.C.

For those who wish to see penguin exhibits in person, the Smithsonian Institution Traveling Exhibition Service (SITES) is bringing "Wondrous Cold: An Antarctic Journey" to audiences nationwide. This exhibit features work from photographer Joan Myers, who spent four months in Antarctica photographing the continent's historical sites, geography, and fauna. Myers's photographs of coastal wildlife include many images of Emperor Penguins near Atka Bay and King Penguins with their chicks, and her visits to historical locations include a trip to the hut occupied by early Antarctic explorer Ernest Shackleton and his team.

For more than 50 years, SITES has been committed to bringing the work of the Smithsonian to the country at large. One of the Smithsonian's four outreach programs, SITES uses items from the Smithsonian archives, as well as audio-visual teaching tools to take entertaining and informative exhibitions to libraries and museums all over the country. "Wondrous Cold" has been on display since May of 2006, and is currently making its way around the United States. The tour is slated to run until June of 2010. For information about "Wondrous Cold" and the SITES program, www.sites.si.edu/.

Admission to the Smithsonian museums is free. The museums are open daily from 10 a.m. to 5:30 p.m. For information about the National Museum of Natural History, call (202) 633-1000, or visit www.si.edu/.

The stunning images of photographer Joan Myers are part of the SITES traveling exhibition "Wondrous Cold: An Antarctic Journey." Shown here are King Penguins and their chicks.

Index

Acknowledgments & Picture Credits

The author wishes to thank Lisa Purcell for her sympathetic and astute touch as an editor, Molly Morrison for providing the opportunity, and his family—Frances, Daniel, and Kelsey—for their support and acceptance that writing comes before renovations.

The author and publisher also offer thanks to those closely involved in the creation of this volume: Christopher Milensky at the National Museum of Natural History; Ellen Nanney, Senior Brand Manager, Katie Mann, and Carolyn Gleason with Smithsonian Business Ventures; Collins Reference executive editor Donna Sanzone, editor Lisa Hacken, and editorial assistant Stephanie Meyers; Hydra Publishing president Sean Moore, publishing director Karen Prince, senior editor/ designer Lisa Purcell, art director Brian MacMullen, designer Erika Lubowicki, production editors Eunho Lee and Anthony Galante, editorial director Aaron Murray, editors Michael Smith, Suzanne Lander, and Rachael Lanicci, picture researcher Ben DeWalt, and indexer Stuart Murray.

PICTURE CREDITS
The following abbreviations are used: SI—Smithsonian Institution; LoC—Library of Congress; PR- Photo Researchers; AP—Associated Press; Wi—Wikimedia; SXG Stock Exchng; iSP—Istockphoto ; NOAA—National Ocean & Atmospheric Aministraton; JI—Jupiter Images; BS—Bigstock Photo; SS—Shutterstock; IO—Index Open; USGS—United States Geological Survey;

(t=top; b=bottom; l=left; r=right; c=center)

Introduction
iii iSP/Thomas O'Neil, iiir IO/Photos.com Select iv–vbg SS/Nik Niklz ivr JI vbc SS/Pascaline Daniel vtr © Adelie Productions vi–1bg SS/Neil Wigmore 1 SS/Geoffrey Whiting 2bl iSP/ Wolfgang Schoenfeld 2tr JI 3 SS/Cre8tive Images

Chapter 1: Penguin History
4 JI 5bg Clipart.com 5r © Adelie Productions 6bl © Adelie Productions 7 © Keith Marshall 8cr SS/Taewoon Lee 8b © Phoebe Chui 9 Clipart.com 10 © Chris Gaskin/Geology Museum, University of Otago 11tr SS/Clara Natoli 11b © Christo Baers/Commonwealth of Australia 2004 12tr SS/ Grigory Kubatyan 12br © Adelie Productions 13 © Phoebe Chui 14tl © Phoebe Chui 14cl © Phoebe Chui 14bl © Phoebe Chui 15tr iSP/Nancy Nehring 15br © Phoebe Chui

Chapter 2: Returning to the Water
16 SS/Vaida 17 © Adelie Productions 18 SS/Joe Gough 19tr iSP/SkyCreative 19br SS/Jan Martin Will 20tl © Adelie Productions 20r SS/Michael Cullen 21cr © Adelie Productions 21b SS/Andrea Leone 22 SS/Silense 23tr SS/Grigory Kubatyan 23br SS/Pascaline Daniel 24 © Adelie Productions 25tr iSP/Lynsey Allan 25br SS/Silense 26 © Adelie Productions 27tl iSP/Kenneth Zirkel 27b SS/Raldi Somers 28 © R. Ewan Fordyce, University of Otago 29tl © Adelie Productions 29br © Phoebe Chui

Chapter 3: Life At Sea
30 SS/Grigory Kubatyan 31 © Adelie Productions 32 SS/ Silense 33tl SS/Nancy Nehring 33bw Wi 34tl SS/Christian Musat 34bl SS/Nicola Gavin 35tl NOAA/Aime Hall 35br iSP/ Frank Vance 36 IO/Anna Zuckerman-Vdovenko 37bl © Adelie Productions 37br © Adelie Productions 38tl SS/Styve Reineck 38bl SS/Latir Keiows 39tl © Phoebe Chui 39tr © Smithsonian Environmental Center 39br © Adelie Productions 40 SS/Raldi Somers 41tr SS/Grigory Kubatyan 41br iSP/Jswax 42tl SS/Ilya D. Gridnev 42bl © Adelie Productions 43tl © Adelie Productions 43br SS/Jan Martin Will 44 JI 45tl BS/ozflash 45br © Adelie Productions

Chapter 4: Finding a Place to Breed
46 © Adelie Productions 47 iSP/Melody Kerchhoff 48cl © Adelie Productions 48br SS/Raldi Somers 49 JI 50 NOAA Corps/Lt. Philip Hall 51tr SS/Silense 51b SS/Pascaline Daniel

52 © Adelie Productions 53tr © Adelie Productions 53br iSP/Roman Kazmin 54 JI 55tr SS/Grigory Kubatyan 55b JI 56tl JI 56br © Adelie Productions 57 © Adelie Productions

Chapter 5: Finding a Mate
58 SS/Silense 59 BS/CristiaCiobanu 60 iSP/Loic Bernard 61tl SXG/Chris Turner 61br © Tourism New Zealand 62 iSP/Melody Kerchhoff 63t © Adelie Productions 63b JI 64bl iSP/Thomas O'Neil 64tr iSP/Melody Kerchhoff 65 SS/Jan Martin Will 66 BS/Mike866 67bl SS/Karl R. Martin 67tr JI 68bl iSP/Margaret and Alan Smeaton 68tr © Adelie Productions 69 iSP/Partick Roherty 70 © Adelie Productions 71 PR/Gregory G. Dimijian 72cl © Adelie Productions 72br SS/H. Tullr 73tl © Adelie Productions 73br SS/Tim Grootkerk 74 JI 75tr SS/Jan Martin Will 75br SS/Coleman Lerner Gerardo 76 © Adelie Productions 77 © Adelie Productions

Chapter 6: Eggs
78 © Adelie Productions 79 © Adelie Productions 80 © Adelie Productions 81tl SS/Silense 81br © Adelie Productions 82bl © Adelie Productions 82tr © Adelie Productions 83 SS/Nik Niklz 84 © Adelie Productions 85tr SS/Davif Hamman 85b SS/Vera Bogaerts 86 © Adelie Productions 87bl © Adelie Productions 87tr © Adelie Productions 88 Wi/Takver 89tl JI 89br © Adelie Productions

Ready Reference
Background: SS/Raldi Somers 90 SS/Jan Marin Will 91 SS/Laitr Keiows 92tl © Adelie Productions 92bc © Adelie Productions 93bl © Adelie Productions 93tr JI 94 JI 95 BS 96bl © Adelie Productions 96tr © Adelie Productions 97 © Matthew Hayward/mathayward.co.uk 98 © Adelie Productions 99 © Adelie Productions 100 © Dave Grady 101 iSP/Heather Faye Bath 102 SS/Alex Balako 103 SS/Luis Cesar Tejo 104bl SS/Hermann Danzmayr 104tr SS/Ritu Manoj Jethani 105 JI

Chapter 7: Chicks
106 © Adelie Productions 107 NOAA/Michael Van Woert 108bl © Adelie Productions 108tr PR/Rod Planck 109cl Public Domain 109br IO/Yvette Cardozo 110 SS/Jose Tejo 111tl SS/Silense 111br © Adelie Productions 112 © Adelie Productions 113t © Adelie Productions 113bl © Adelie Productions 113cr © Adelie Productions 114 iSP/Alexander Kautz 115t © Adelie Productions 115br © Adelie Productions 116 SS/Coleman Lerner Gerardo 117tl © Adelie Productions 117br SS/Pascaline Daniel 118 © Adelie Productions 119tl © Adelie Productions 119br © Adelie Productions 120 SS/Mike Pluth 121t © Adelie Productions 121br SS/Silense

Chapter 8: Behavior
122 © Adelie Productions 123 IO/Photos.com Select 124 © Adelie Productions 125 © Adelie Productions 126 iSP/Chris Crafter 127 © Adelie Productions 128 JI 129tl SS/Adrian Jones 129br JI 130 JI 131tl © Adelie Productions 131br PR/Rod Planck 132 © Adelie Productions 133bl © Adelie Productions 133tr © Adelie Productions

Chapter 9: Molt
134 © Adelie Productions 135 IO/Vostock, LLC 136 SS/Derrick den Hollander 137 © Adelie Productions 138 iSP/Ronald Kools 138 iSP/Vera Bogaerts 140 © Adelie Productions 141 © Adelie Productions 142 iSP/Allison Murray 143 PR/Gregory Dimijian 144 SS/Tim Hope 145 JI

Chapter 10: Migration
146 © Adelie Productions 147 iSP/Melody Kerchhoff 148 © Adelie Productions 149 SS/Vera Bogaerts 150 SPL/William Curtsinger 151tr iSP/Jean-Yves Benedyt 151br © Diane Moyle 152 USGS/Ken Farke 153bl © Adelie Productions 153tr SS/Cristi Matei 154 SS/Fsquared 155 PR/Gregory Dimijian 156bl BS/Gfadel 156br SS/SG James 157 iSP/Armin Rose 158bl SS/Styve Reineck 158tr © Ryan Hagerty, U.S. Fish and Wildlife Service 159 AP/Obed Zilwa 160 iSP/Wolfgang Shoenfeld 161bl SS/Eric Gevaert 161tr iSP/Wolfgang Shoenfeld

Chapter 11: Penguins and People
162 AP/News LTD. 163 iSP/Katie Winegarden 164bl SS/Xiao Li 164tr © Larry Ewing, Simon Budig, Anja Gerwinski 165 iSP/Bobby Aquitania 166 © Scott Polar Research Institute 167tr NOAA 167b SS/Silense 168 SS/Rebecca Picard 169t iSP/Chee Kong See Thoe 169b SS/Christoffer Vika 170 JI 171tr iSP/Lisa Vanovitch 171b SS/Joy Brown 172tl NOAA 172br iSP/Tammy Belanger 173tl © Adelie Productions 173br NOAA 174 AP/IFAW, Jon Hrusa 175tr SS/Steven Hampshire 175bc Wi 176bl Morguefile/Clarita 176tr SS/Xavier Marchant 177tl iSP/Jose Tejo 177br ACME Co. 178 AP/NASA 179 © Adelie Productions 180 IO/Anna Zuckerman-Vdovenko 181tr © Adelie Productions 181b iSP/Loic Bernard

Chapter 12: Penguins at Risk
182 iSP/Oscar Schnell 183 JI 184 SS/Jan Martin Will 185 JI 186 © Otago Daily Times 187 JI 188 SS/Yuriy Maskymenko 189bl BS/Seraphic 189br SS/David Swomley 190 © Adelie Productions 191 © Falklands Conservation Penguin Census 2000/01 192bl SS/James Steidl 192tr SS/Vera Bogaerts 193 © Adelie Productions 194cl LOC/Louise Welsh 194br SS/Andrea Leone 195tr SS/Steven Ringelr 195br iSP/Michael Rolands 196cl Public Domain 196br Public Domain 197tr Public Domain 197cr © National Library of Australia 198 SS/Vera Bogaerts 199 © Adelie Productions 200 Morguefile/ Clarita 201 AP/Tourism of New Zealand 202 © Adelie Productions 203 K. Sado, University of California at San Diego

Further Reading
206 NOAA/Michael Van Woert 207 © Adelie Productions

At the Smithsonian
208 SI/Dane A. Penland 209 © Joan Myers

Front cover images:
Clockwise from top right: JI, iSP/Thomas O'Neil, IO/Photos.com Select

Back cover images:
Top: MF/Ripert Jefferies Bottom: JI